70th Congress, 2d Session - - - House Document No. 551

PROPOSED AMENDMENTS

TO THE

CONSTITUTION

A MONOGRAPH ON THE
RESOLUTIONS INTRODUCED IN CONGRESS
PROPOSING AMENDMENTS TO THE CONSTITUTION
OF THE UNITED STATES OF AMERICA

GREENWOOD PRESS, PUBLISHERS
WESTPORT, CONNECTICUT

Library of Congress Cataloging in Publication Data

Musmanno, Michael Angelo.
Proposed amendments to the Constitution.

Reprint of the 1929 ed. published by the U. S. Govt. Print. Off., Washington, in series: United States. Congress. House. Document no. 551.
1. United States. Constitution—Amendments. I. Title. II. Series: United States. 70th Congress, 2d session, 1928-1929. House. Document ; no. 551.
KF4557.M8 1976 342'.73'03 75-35374
ISBN 0-8371-8610-2

Originally published in 1929 by United States Government Printing Office, Washington

Reprinted in 1976 by Greenwood Press, a division of Williamhouse-Regency Inc.

Library of Congress Catalog Card Number 75-35374

ISBN 0-8371-8610-2

Printed in the United States of America

HOUSE RESOLUTION NO. 82

Submitted by Mr. Kelly

IN THE HOUSE OF REPRESENTATIVES,
January 9, 1928.

Resolved, That the compilation made by M. A. Musmanno from the Congressional Record of the facts regarding all amendments of the Constitution of the United States proposed since 1889 be printed as a public document.

Attest:

WILLIAM TYLER PAGE,
Clerk.

PREFACE

In 1899 Prof. Herman V. Ames published a treatise on the 1,300 amendments introduced in Congress during the first 100 years of the Constitution's history. Since then, or in only 39 years, another 1,300 amendments have been presented (1,370, to be exact), a fact capable of much interpretation. Professor Ames's treatise was never extended to embrace these latter resolutions, so that prior to the publication of this work there was nothing in the field which would give students of governmental affairs an up-to-date comprehensive idea on this most phenomenal phase of constitutional activity and development.

Although in this monograph I treat particularly the amendments introduced since 1889, such being the main burden of the work, yet I include in every section of the text a brief and succinct account of the amendments proposed from 1789 to 1889, if any were presented on the subject under discussion in that particular section. In this way I have endeavored to achieve a certain unity in the work, so that at a moment's glance one may tell what has been the trend of the times on each particular phase of Constitution amending since 1789, which year is now definitely established as the date of the real beginning of the American Commonwealth.

M. A. Musmanno.

CONTENTS

Chapter I

PROPOSED AMENDMENTS AFFECTING THE FORM OF GOVERNMENT: LEGISLATIVE

	Page
1. Changing the time of the sessions of Congress	1
2. Extra and biennial sessions	9
3. Election of Representatives	10
4. Apportionment of Representatives	13
5. Term of Representatives	17
6. Permitting Members of Congress to hold seats in the President's Cabinet	19
7. Terms of Senators	20
8. Rules of the Senate	20

Chapter II

PROPOSED AMENDMENTS AFFECTING THE FORM OF GOVERNMENT: EXECUTIVE

9. Changing date of Inauguration Day	23
10. Presidential electors	44
11. Election of President and Vice President by a general direct vote; also general electoral vote	45
12. Term of the President and Vice President	51
13. Presidential self-succession	53
14. One-term Presidency	55
15. Six-year presidential term	57
16. Settlement of contested presidential elections	60
17. The question of ex-Presidents	64
18. The veto power	67
19. Power of removal	71

Page

20. Election of Executive officials 72
21. Abolition of life tenure 72
22. Pertaining to the Presidency 74
23. Succession to the Presidency 76
24. Vice Presidents 80

CHAPTER III

PROPOSED AMENDMENTS AFFECTING THE FORM OF GOVERNMENT: JUDICIARY

25. Term of judges 82
26. Removal of judges 84
27. Election of judges 86
28. Judges to be ineligible to other offices 87
29. Composition of courts 88
30. Jurisdiction of the courts 88
31. Power of the Supreme Court to declare laws unconstitutional 92

CHAPTER IV

PROPOSED AMENDMENTS AFFECTING THE POWERS OF THE GOVERNMENT

32. Powers of Congress 96
33. Bearing of weapons 100
34. Impeachment 100
35. Land legislation 101
36. Marriage and divorce 104
37. Divorces 106
38. Miscegenation 108
39. Money 109
40. Export duties 111
41. Import duties 112
42. Trusts and monopolies 114
43. Protection of trade-marks 119
44. The treaty-making power 120
45. War powers 124
46. The Army 126

	Page
47. The militia	127
48. Military pensions	129
49. Prohibition of polygamy	131
50. Protection to labor	135
51. Child labor	137
52. Lotteries	145
53. Insurance	146
54. Treason	147

Limitations on powers of Congress

55. Prohibition of special legislation	149
56. Expenditures—appropriation bills	150
57. Claims against the United States	151
58. Chartering corporations	152

Territorial powers

59. Admission of Territories into the United States	154
60. The District of Columbia	157

Federal taxation

61. Direct taxes	161
62. Inheritance taxes	163
63. Taxation of State securities, Federal and State officers, and stock dividends	164
64. Taxation of corporations by States	171
65. Uniformity of taxation and capitation tax	171

Initiative, referendum, and recall

66. The initiative, referendum, and recall	172
67. The initiative and referendum	173
68. The recall	176

The question of aliens

69. Right to vote at Federal elections	177
70. Japanese aliens	180

Page
71. Excluding States from consideration of alien questions.... 181
72. Religion.... 182
73. Recognizing the Deity in the Constitution.... 183
74. Proposition to change the name of the country.... 185
75. Cumulative voting.... 186
76. Fortunes.... 187

Chapter V

PROCEDURE AS TO CONSTITUTIONAL AMENDMENTS

77. Early proposals on this subject.... 189
78. Recent attempts to change Article V.... 191
79. Changing majorities required for congressional proposals, calling of conventions, and ratifications.... 192
80. Senator La Follette's plan.... 194
81. Senator Owen's plan.... 195
82. Senator Cummins's plan.... 196
83. Initiative amendments.... 197
84. Ratification by popular vote.... 199
85. Length of time in which ratification may be made.... 204

Chapter VI

AMENDMENTS XIV TO XIX

86. The fourteenth amendment.... 207
87. The fifteenth amendment.... 209
88. Income tax amendment.... 210
89. Direct election of Senators.... 215
90. Amendments introduced to effect popular election of Senators.... 218
91. The seventeenth amendment.... 219
92. The prohibition amendment.... 225
93. History of prohibition in the United States.... 226
94. Prohibition legislation in Congress.... 228
95. Attempts made to add a prohibition amendment to the Constitution.... 230
96. The eighteenth amendment.... 233

CONTENTS

Page

97. Repeal of the prohibition amendment.................. 237
98. Woman suffrage.. 242
99. History of the suffrage movement in the States.......... 243
100. Woman suffrage in the National Legislature............. 246
101. Arguments for and against a Federal suffrage amendment.. 248
102. The nineteenth amendment.............................. 251
103. Equal rights of women.................................. 253

Chapter I

PROPOSED AMENDMENTS AFFECTING THE FORM OF GOVERNMENT: LEGISLATIVE

1. Changing the time of the sessions of Congress.

What are the most feasible dates for the beginning and ending of Congress? This is a proposition which has engaged the attention of legislators since the first days of the Republic. The Constitution states that Congress shall meet on the first Monday in December every year (Art. I, sec. 4, cl. 2), but does not specify when the terms of the Members shall begin and terminate.

On September 12, 1788, the Continental Congress launched the new Constitution by a resolution which read:[1]

> *Resolved,* That the first Wednesday in January next be the day for appointing electors in the several States; that the first Wednesday in February next be the day for the electors to assemble in their several States and vote for President, and that the first Wednesday in March next be the time and the present seat of Congress the place for commencing the proceedings under the said Constitution.

The first Wednesday of March fell on the 4th and thus the Members of Congress began their term of office on that date. Serving for two years, the term prescribed by the Constitution (Art. I, sec. 2, cl. 1) their term expired March 4, 1791, so March 4 accordingly became the official date of the ending of each Congress. That this date was not wholly satisfactory is evidenced by the fact that as early as 1795 an amendment was introduced to change

[1] Journal of Continental Congress, Vol. IV, p. 867.

the term of Congress so as to have it end June 1. In 1808 a resolution was presented providing that Congress should sit for but one year and that the term should expire on the first Tuesday in April. In 1840 a resolution declaring December 1 as the commencement of the term of Members was proposed. From 1876 to 1889, 18 amendments were introduced covering the subject of time of the sessions of Congress.[2] From 1889 to 1928, 93 attempts have been made to alter the beginning and ending dates of Congress; 10 of the resolutions provided that the congressional term, with the presidential should begin and end on April 30 instead of March 4;[3] 19 others extended the terms to the last Wednesday or Thursday in April;[4] 1 gave the first Tuesday in May as the pivotal date for the presidential and congressional terms, and 1 March 30.[5]

The others provided that Congress should assemble immediately after the election, 1 indicating the first Monday in October as the beginning date of each Congress;[6] 1 the first Monday of November;[7] another the first Monday in December following the election;[8] and 59 giving some day in the first or second week in January.[9]

---

[2]Ames, Const., Amendments, p. 36.

[3]App., Nos. 5, 10, 23, 24, 85, 215, 240, 333, 376, 569.

[4]App., Nos. 285, 318, 340, 351, 368, 430, 431, 518, 519, 521, 532,

[5]App., Nos. 520, 553.

[6] App., No. 471.

557, 567, 571, 582, 603, 612, 613, 686.

[7] App., No. 1096.

[8] App., No. 1028.

[9]App., Nos. 26, 28, 31, 98, 80, 92, 97, 125, 410, 435, 437, 467, 482, 556a, 570, 625, 592, 696, 697, 746, 777, 792, 799, 858, 896, 1029, 1043, 1052, 1129, 1136, 1146, 1170, 1171, 1181, 1184, 1189, 1208, 1209, 1215, 1216, 1233, 1257, 1269, 1272, 1275, 1278, 1284, 1288, 1289, 1309, 1317, 1318, 1323, 1333, 1340, 1344, 1351, 1362.

The primary objection made by those desiring a change in the beginning date of Congress is that, as now constituted, it does not actually begin until 13 months after the members thereof have been elected. It thus frequently happens that issues upon which they have been elected have been settled by the old Congress or put into such a condition as to make adjustment doubly difficult.[10] For nine months there is no speaker of the House and the shortness of the second session often prevents the passage of important measures.[11] It is also claimed that Congressmen who have been defeated for reelection have the opportunity during the session after the election to vote, without responsibility, for private legislation in which they will secure some personal gain.[12]

From 1886 to 1893, Mr. Crain, from Texas, introduced 11 resolutions seeking to amend the Constitution so as to make December 31, instead of March 4, the beginning and termination of the official term of Members of the House of Representatives and Senate, and providing that

[10] H. Rept. No. 543, 52d Cong., 1st sess. This report states: The Republicans carried the congressional election in 1888 while the Democrats were victorious in 1890, yet the Mills Congress in one instance and the McKinley Congress in the other continued to legislate for the country although repudiated at the polls.

[11] H. Rept. No. 543, 52d Cong., 1st sess. This report states: Due to lack of time the deficiency bill of the 2d session, Forty-ninth Congress, failed of passage.

[12] Beard, American Government and Politics, p. 249. Mr. Shafroth, an ex-Congressman, speaking of the second session, said: "It is then that some are open to propositions which they would never think of entertaining if they were to go before the people for reelection. It is then that the attorneyship of some corporation is often tendered, and a vote is afterward found in the Record in favor of legislation of a general or special character favoring corporations."

Congress should hold its annual meetings on the first Monday in January.[13]

On April 30, 1892, the House Committee on Election of President, Vice President, and Representatives in Congress, with a complete unanimity, favorably reported one of these Crain resolutions (H. Res. 98).[14] Speaking on the resolution, Mr. Crain pointed out that a constitutional amendment, and not merely a law, is needed to change the term, because the action of the convention ratified by the Congress has fixed it as a part of the Constitution that the terms of the Members of Congress begin on the 4th of March and terminate on March 4.[15]

Mr. Hooker, of Mississippi, was in favor of the ends to be attained by the amendment, but by reason of the great delay attendant upon the ratification of a constitutional amendment maintained that the same results could be achieved through a law by merely changing the date Congress is to meet from the first Monday in December to the first Monday after the 4th day of March. This would give two sessions of equal length with no considerable gap between the election day and the swearing in of the new Members. He introduced a bill to this effect (H. R. 9731).[16]

Mr. Cochran, of New York, opposing the joint resolution, stated that it would be highly unwise to have any presidential contest decided by a Congress that was elected at the same time with the President. This is what would happen should the election of the President devolve upon the House of Representatives, for under this new scheme

---

[13] Ames, p. 37. App., Nos. 24, 26, 31, 98, 80, 97, 125.

[14] App., No. 98. H. Rept. No. 98, 52d Cong., 1st sess.

[15] Cong. Rec., Jan. 10, 1893, vol. 24, pt. 1, p. 485.

[16] Ibid., p. 487.

the new Congress would meet in January and the President would be inaugurated in April. Had this system been in effect in 1876, in the famous Hayes-Tilden contest, the " same forces that had raised the dispute about succession to the Presidency would have been able to foment disputes about the complexion of the new Congress, so that you would have had two Congresses competing for regularity." [17]

Mr. Reed, of Maine, also opposed, declared that our system of government did not intend an immediate response to the opinion of the people but that our " institutions are formed upon the idea that the careful determination of the people of the United States well stuck to shall be the law of the land; not the opinion of one election; but the opinion of a series of elections." [18] On January 10, 1893, the resolution was put to a vote and failed of passage, 49 yeas to 128 nays.[19]

In introducing Senate Joint Resolution No. 83 on January 14, 1898, Senator Hoar, of Massachusetts, pointed out that omitting the Christmas holidays and Sundays there were only about 65 days left for business in the short session, too short a time for the proper consideration of any but the great appropriation bills, of which there were 13. On the other hand, the first session of each Congress, on account of the volume of business to be transacted, was prolonged for 6, 7, or 8 months. He proposed to amend the Constitution so as to substitute April 30 for March 4 as the official date for the beginning and termination of the congressional term, thus equalizing the work of the two sessions by taking away some of the

[17] Cong. Rec., Jan. 10, 1893, vol. 24, pt. 1, p. 489.

[18] Ibid., p. 495.

[19] Ibid., p. 499.

burden of the first and adding it to the second.[20] His resolution passed the Senate May 10, 1898,[21] and was referred to the House Committee on Judiciary,[22] from which it did not emerge.

The argument advanced by Senator Hoar in the consideration of Senate Joint Resolution No. 83 with regard to the shortness of the second session was answered by Mr. Driscoll, of New York, in the consideration of House Joint Resolution No. 115 in the Sixty-first Congress. He claimed that the time intervening between the first Monday in December and the 4th of March was sufficient in which to pass the supply bills, and " that is about all that Congress, composed of many Members who are really not responsible to their constituents, should do. When the Members are still in office and hope for reelection, and when they are more inclined to be responsive to the wishes of their constituents is the time for constructive laws and new legislation." [23] This resolution (H. J. Res. No. 115), was introduced by Mr. Henry, of Texas, and provided for the last Thursday in April as the pivotal date for the presidential and congressional terms. On January 15, 1910, it was recommitted to the Committee on Judiciary and was reported back under House Joint Resolution No. 174,[24] for which it was substituted. On May 16, 1910, it came to a vote, and lacking the necessary two-thirds majority, the resolution was lost, 138 yeas to 72 nays.[25]

Senate Joint Resolution No. 10, providing for the first Monday in January as the official date for the beginning

[20] Cong. Rec., May 10, 1898, p. 4763.

[21] Ibid., p. 4772.

[22] Ibid., p. 4827.

[23] Cong. Rec., Jan. 14, 1910, p. 646.

[24] H. Rept. No. 369, Mar. 16, 1910, 61st Cong., 2d sess.

[25] Cong. Rec., May 16, 1910, p. 6368.

and ending of the congressional term, and the second Monday in January for the presidential term, introduced in 1913 by Senator Shafroth, of Colorado, was unfavorably reported by the Committee on Judiciary.[26] The minority members of the committee reported the need of such a change, declaring that with Congress not meeting until 13 months after its election, "it is unfair to the administration that the legislation which it thinks so essential to the prosperity of the country should be so long deferred." The call of an extraordinary session does not meet the difficulty, since it is usually limited to the consideration of one or two subjects which "make enormous waste of time of each House, waiting for the other to consider and pass the measure." The minority further criticized the present system by referring to the contests over seats in the House of Representatives. They declared that decisions on these contests are seldom given until about one-half of the term has expired, and sometimes as much as 22 months. For all this time the occupant draws the salary and when his opponent is seated he also draws the salary for the full term, so that the Government pays twice and the district is misrepresented. With "Congress meeting the first Monday in January succeeding the election, contested-election cases could be disposed of at least during the first six months of the Congress." [27] This resolution was finally passed over without a vote.

From the above it seems that some change in the dates of the congressional terms is desired, but there is a great variety of opinions as to what constitutes the best change. In the discussion of House Joint Resolution No. 174, in 1910, Mr. Parker, of New Jersey, said that he preferred

26 S. Rept. No. 212, 63d Cong., 1st sess.

27 S. Rept. No. 212, 63d Cong., 1st sess., App., No. 690.

the House to meet in December, the Senate in March, and the President to be inaugurated in April, but since it was so difficult to get a consensus of favorable opinion on such a variety of dates he was willing to accept the last Thursday in April as the pivotal date for the congressional and the presidential terms.[28] This would add six or seven weeks to the present short session, and if necessary Congress could arrange by law to meet in the latter part of November instead of the first Monday in December and thus make the last session of each Congress of sufficient length to properly weigh all matters which may come before it.

The objection against having Congress meet immediately after an election—i. e., within two or three months—rests mainly on the theory that good legislation depends upon deliberation and that there is a dangerous tendency in having new Members fresh from the speeches and excitement of a campaign make laws that are to remain permanently on the statute books of the Nation.[29] There is also the opinion that should a presidential election be thrown into the House of Representatives for decision that it is better to have the Members of a preceding Congress determine the choice rather than the Members of a new Congress whose right to sit may be questioned as much as the authority of the presidential electors.[30]

During the last four Congresses (67th, 68th, 69th, and 70th) four resolutions effecting a change in the beginning date of Congress passed the Senate with large majori-

[28] Cong. Rec., Mar. 16, 1910, p. 3264.

[29] H. Rept. No. 769, 55th Cong., 2d sess.

[30] Cong. Rec., Jan. 10, 1893, pp. 483–500.

ties.[31] Only one of them came to a vote in the House (S. J. Res. 47; 70th Congress), and it failed of passage. These resolutions (67th Congress, S. J. Res. 253; 68th Congress, S. J. Res. 22; 69th Congress, S. J. Res. 9; 70th Congress, S. J. Res. 47) are discussed in section 9.[32]

2. Extra and biennial sessions.

It was for a long time accepted in American politics that in order to have good government the legislatures ought to assemble frequently. Lately, however, the pendulum has been swinging the other way, and we thus find that although originally all the State legislatures met at least once a year, 41 of the 48 States now provide for but biennial sessions, while one State—Alabama—has quadrennial sessions.[33] This curtailment in legislative activity has not as yet been felt in the national legislature, and only two resolutions have so far been introduced in Congress attempting to make its sessions biennial. One was introduced in 1878 [34] and the other in 1892.[35] The latter provided that Congress should " assemble at least once in every two years," thus allowing for additional sessions if needed.

In 1873 President Grant recommended to Congress the passage of an amendment limiting extra sessions of Con-

[31] S. J. Res. 253 passed with a vote of 63 to 6; S. J. Res. 22 passed with a vote of 63 to 7; S. J. Res. 9 passed with a vote of 73 to 2; S. J. Res. 47 passed with a vote of 67 to 6.

[32] P. 26.

[33] Beard, American Government and Politics, p. 528. Only six of the States now provide for annual meetings of the legislature. They are: Georgia, Massachusetts, New Jersey, New York, Rhode Island, and South Carolina.

[34] Ames, p. 38.

[35] App., No. 96.

gress to the consideration of only such matters as are brought to its attention by the President, but there is no record that any such amendment was introduced.[36] In the Fifty-ninth and Sixtieth Congresses Mr. De Armond, of Missouri, presented a resolution providing that Congress should meet on the first Monday in January of each year and that no Congress should "sit after the general election for Representatives in the succeeding Congress except when convened in extraordinary session, and then shall be confined to the matters embraced in the proclamation calling such extraordinary session." [37] The matter of doing away with extra sessions by a rearrangement of the annual sessions has been discussed in the preceding section.

3. Election of Representatives.

The power of Congress to make regulations concerning the election of Representatives has not been extensively exercised, only a few laws having been passed under this authority. In 1842 election of Representatives by districts was made mandatory; in 1871 Congress passed a law requiring all candidates for Congress to be voted for on written or printed ballots, and in 1872 the uniform election day law was put into effect.[38]

The Constitution permits the respective States to determine the qualifications of the electors choosing the Members for the National House of Representatives by making those qualifications to agree with the "qualifications requisite for electors of the most numerous branch

[36]Ames, p. 38.
[37]App., Nos. 437, 467.
[38]Ames, p. 58.

of the State legislature." [39] As the State has sovereign power in prescribing the qualifications for electors of the State legislature, the State could if it desired require unreasonable qualifications of an elector before allowing him the suffrage, thus affecting the election of Representatives to Congress. There is no indication that any State would deprive itself of proper representation in its own legislature in order to effect a material change in the qualifications requisite for electors of Representatives to Congress, but apparently to obviate any possible trend in this direction, Mr. Smith, of Michigan, has on two occasions (1901 and 1902) introduced an amendment providing that Congress shall have power to determine the qualifications requisite for electors of Members to the House of Representatives, which qualifications shall be uniform throughout the United States.[40]

Three amendments, proposed, respectively, in 1921, 1922, and 1923, lead away from Federal interposition in that they provide that when vacancies occur in the representation of any State the executive authority thereof may make temporary appointments until the next general election.[41]

An amendment of this nature would undoubtedly be quite beneficial, since, by reason of the great expense attendant upon special elections for replacements in Congress, it frequently happens that a State would rather go without its full representation. For instance, as was declared in House Report No. 706, Sixty-seventh Congress, which recommended the passage of one of these

[39] U. S. Const., Art. I, sec. 2.

[40] App., Nos. 317, 360.

[41] App., Nos. 1074, 1094, 1201.

resolutions (H. J. Res. No. 252), " when vacancies happen by death or resignation of a Congressman at Large, especially in a very large State, such as Pennsylvania or Illinois, the expense of a special election is well-nigh prohibitive. Such vacancies in Illinois and Pennsylvania may be cited as recent occurrences. Pennsylvania failed to elect for a consilerable period of time, or until a regular election appeared." [42]

On December 15, 1927, Mr. Wilson, of Mississippi, introduced a resolution providing that only natural-born citizens may be Senators or Representatives.[43]

The disclosures of the large amounts of money spent in the spring of 1926 in various primaries throughout the county led Mr. Rubey, of Missouri, to introduce a resolution to the effect that no person shall be a Representative if the aggregate expenditures made by him or with his knowledge and consent for his nomination and election exceed $5,000. The resolution includes a similar provision for Senators, the limit there being $10,000.[44]

On April 18, 1928, Mr. Rathbone, of Illinois, introduced a resolution providing that Congress shall have power to regulate and limit contributions and expenditures made to and for candidates for party nominations for all elective Federal offices.[45]

Senator Cutting, of New Mexico, submitted an amendment that any candidate for the office of Representative or Senator who violated congressional laws regarding nomination and election would be ineligible for election.[46]

[42] 67th Cong., H. Rept. No. 706.
[43] App., No. 1337.
[44] App., No. 1297.
[45] App., No. 1354.
[46] App., No. 1357.

Senator Cutting introduced two further amendments on the subject during the Seventieth Congress giving Congress power to legislate and prevent fraud and corrupt practices in the nomination and election of Senators. Representatives, President and Vice President.[47]

4. Apportionment of Representatives.

Since 1889, 12 attempts have been made to amend the Constitution so as to limit the membership of the House of Representatives to a certain number.[48] Each census, except that of 1840, has occasioned an increase in the House membership, and in recent years the opinion has gathered force that this body is becoming too unwieldy for the most efficient transaction of public business.

This theory was probably the cause for the four amendments introduced in the third session of the Sixty-sixth Congress when, through the census of 1920, the great increase in the population was made manifest.[49] And it was perhaps the possibility of such an amendment actually being approved that led Mr. Dale, of Vermont, to introduce a resolution (H. J. Res. 399) providing that every State should be entitled to at least two Representatives, thus forestalling any restricted membership which would give the smaller States but the one Representative guaranteed in the Constitution.[50] (Art. I, sec. 3.) Three similar resolutions have been introduced since.[51]

Fear has also been expressed that with the great increase in numbers in the House of Representatives the

[47] App., No. 1355.

[48] App., Nos. 46, 230, 316, 319, 358, 407, 575, 1025, 1032, 1033, 1034.

[49] App., Nos. 1025, 1932, 1033, 1034, 1050.

[50] App., No. 1026.

[51] App., Nos. 1207, 1218, 1261.

Government will become more national than Federal and thus subvert the intention of the framers of the Constitution.[52]

Those who do not believe in a restricted membership contend that the public business of the country is such as to require a large House of Representatives. In adjusting the apportionment on the basis of the census of 1920 providing for an increase of 35 Members, the House Committee on the Census showed that with a population of 105,708,771 the ratio of representation would be 1 representative for every 228,882 people. (The ratio previous to this was 211,877.) Considering also on the basis of 4,600,000 men having served in the World War under American colors, this distributes to each Representative an ex-service constituency of about 10,000, which always takes up a great deal of a Representative's time.[53]

A large membership is also needed to properly operate the many committees. It is well understood that most of the work of any Congress is now done in these committees, and " in view of the requests by the people for different kinds of laws, it is becoming self-evident that the Members will soon find themselves in the position that they will only be able to serve on one committee in order to become experts of the particular subject which the committee is handling." [54]

The various resolutions introduced to restrict the House membership vary as to the maximum figure, the limited number ranging from 200 to 500, with the provision that if other States are admitted to the Union they shall be

[52] Ames, p. 55.

[53] H. Rept. No. 312, 67th Cong., 1st sess.

[54] H. Rept. No. 313, 67th Cong., 1st sess.

entitled to one Representative each until the next Congress when a reapportionment will be made among all the States according to population.

House Joint Resolution No. 253 introduced in the Sixty-first Congress by Mr. Foelker, of New York, providing for a House membership of 400, included the unusual provision of cumulative voting, stipulating that on every matter coming before the House of Representatives every Representative should have one vote for each 10,000 votes cast for him in the district which elected him.[55]

An amendment introduced by Senator Jones, of Washington, in 1916 provided that Representatives should be apportioned according to the numerical strength of the various vocations of the electors.[56] This amendment was probably actuated by the oft-heard criticism that there are too many lawyers in Congress and not enough representatives of the other vocations. This amendment was reintroduced in 1921.[57]

In 1919, Senator Sherman, of Illinois, introduced an amendment stipulating that the suffrage should be granted to all those (regardless of sex) who could read and write English. As an inducement to the States to encourage the education of illiterates and to urge the women to vote, there was added the provision that each State's apportionment of Representatives would be based upon the ratio the State vote bore to the entire national vote in the congressional election next preceding.[58]

Two amendments introduced in 1921, one in 1925, and another in 1927, designed to have congressional represen-

[55]App., No. 575.
[56]App., No. 844.
[57]App., No. 1067.
[58]App., Nos. 993, 1332.

tation based upon actual voting strength rather than potential voting power, provided that representatives shall be apportioned according to the votes counted at the presidential election next preceding the decennial census.[59]

On December 10, 1927, Mr. Stalker, of New York, introduced (by request) a resolution providing that aliens shall be excluded in counting the whole number of persons in each State for apportionment of Representatives.[60]

In order evidently to avoid any delay in the reapportionment of Representatives according to the new censuses, two resolutions were presented in 1924, declaring that at the conclusion of each decennial enumeration the President shall note the result and notify the several States of the number of Representatives to which each is entitled.[61] One introduced in 1925 declared that the apportioning and notifying power shall devolve upon Congress.[62]

Another resolution presented in 1921, looking to the future, provided that beginning with the Seventy-seventh Congress the unit of population for each member shall be one three-hundredths of the population of all the States as determined by the census of 1930. It provided further that in 1970 and every 30 years thereafter upon the request of not less than one-half of the States and upon the admission of a new State, the unit of population was to be redetermined according to the last preceding census.[63]

In 1921 a resolution was presented declaring that Congress shall have power to fix and determine the congres-

[59]App., Nos. 1051, 1066, 1269, 1322.
[60]App., No. 1336.
[61]App., Nos. 1222, 1223.
[62]App., No. 1254.
[63]App., No. 1088.

sional representation overseas and noncontiguous territory now or to be hereafter acquired.[64]

5. Term of Representatives.

From 1789 to 1869 only two attempts were made to change the term of Members of the House of Representatives, one to decrease it to one year and the other to prevent any person from serving more than six years in any term of eight years.[65] From 1869 to 1928, 21 resolutions have been introduced to increase the term to three years; [66] 37 to increase the term to four years; [67] and 3 to six years.[68] Three of these resolutions, one providing for a 4-year term and two for a 6-year term, included a provision making the Representatives subject to recall by their electors.[69] One other resolution providing for the recall of Congressmen was presented in 1907.[70]

The arguments advanced in favor of a longer term for Representatives are that the term of office, as at present constituted, has practically half expired before the Members take the oath; that shortly after this takes place their efforts in Congress are dissipated by the campaign at home for renomination and then later for reelection; that if defeated they are apt to take little interest in the business of the second session; and that if reelected there is

[64]App., No. 1059.

[65]Ames, p. 60.

[66]Ames, p. 60. App., Nos. 38, 88, 140, 204, 309, 410, 435, 494, 618, 635, 777, 790, 923.

[67]Ames, p. 60. App., Nos. 201, 205, 207, 262, 280, 408, 423, 441, 504, 559, 564, 600, 610, 663, 707, 745, 746, 809, 811, 821, 833, 884, 910, 944, 1086, 1088, 1096, 1125, 1146, 1209, 1251, 1259, 1285, 1359.

[68]Ames, p. 60, App., Nos. 735, 790.

[69]App., Nos. 735, 790, 884.

[70]App., No. 477.

the possibility of their sense of security being too great for efficiency. It is also maintained by the advocates of a longer term that the frequency of elections coupled with the expense of a campaign makes it impossible for a poor man to retain his seat and that for this reason many of the most able and efficient Members are continually withdrawing from office.[71]

Contra, it is contended that the Representatives should be kept close to the people and this can best be done by frequency of elections. As stated by one opponent of any change:

> Hold the whip hand over your Member of Congress. If he indicates by his service in Congress he is a worthy man, you can keep him there; but if the least suspicion crops out that you are deceived in your Member of Congress, keep it in your power to make a change at the first and shortest time possible.[72]

Members in Congress adhering to the present plan say that the people are not demanding any increasing of the terms of Members of the House of Representatives, and that when they do it will be time enough to effect a change.[73]

On June 20, 1906, a vote was taken on the proposition of a 4-year term for Representatives, but the result can not be taken as conclusive indication of the attitude of the House at that time for the reason that it was coupled up with the provision for the popular election of Senators. It was claimed by some that the section providing for a 4-year term for Representatives was purposely joined to the popular election for Senator clause in order to insure

[71] H. Rept. No. 3165, 59th Cong., 1st sess.

[72] Mr. Gilbert, of Kentucky. Cong. Rec., June 20, 1906, p. 8829.

[73] Cong. Rec., 59th Cong., 1st sess. See discussion pp. 5108, 8827, 8832.

its passage, the latter proposition having passed the House four different times by a practically unanimous vote. A futile effort being made at the last moment to divide the question, the entire resolution failed on a vote of 89 ayes to 86 noes.[74]

During the Sixty-seventh and Sixty-eighth Congresses, seven resolutions were presented providing for a 4-year term for Congressmen. Five of these declared that the entire membership of the House should be elected every four years.[75] whereas two provided that one-half of the membership should be renewed every two years.[76] One of these resolutions (H. J. Res. 220, 67th Cong.) was recommended favorably by the Committee on the Election of President, Vice President, and Representatives in Congress, but did not reach a vote in the House.

6. Permitting Members of Congress to hold seats in the President's Cabinet.

Three attempts have so far been made to remove the inhibition in Article I, section 6, clause 2, of the Constitution which prohibits a Senator or Representative from holding any other office under the United States while still a Member of Congress.[77] If amended according to any of these resolutions the Constitution would permit a Member of Congress to be appointed to the President's Cabinet and still retain his seat in the legislature. This is the English system and it is declared has its advantages in that it allows the legislators to come into more frequent contact with the heads of the departments and thus

[74] Cong. Rec., June 20, 1906, p. 8832.

[75] App., Nos. 1086, 1088, 1125, 1146, 1209.

[76] App., Nos. 1096, 1251.

[77] App., Nos. 202, 209, 264.

become better informed as to the needs of these departments of the government. There is the further reputed advantage in that it would furnish active leaders in Congress for the purpose of initiating legislation recommended by the President.

7. Terms of Senators.

From 1789 to 1839, eight amendments were introduced to reduce the senatorial term—some to one, some to three, and some to four years.[78] During the first part of our constitutional history there was always the fear that too long a tenure might develop an aloofness from the people and a disregarding of the political and civic needs of the time. These fears, however, have apparently been put to rest and thus no further attempt has been made to decrease the senatorial term. On the contrary, in 1896 Mr. Treloar, of Missouri, introduced a resolution (H. Res. 208) providing that the term of a Senator shall be eight years instead of six years.[79] This was in conjunction with the plan for increasing the President's term to eight years with no reeligibility, and the Representative's term to four years. Mr. Norris, of Nebraska, introduced a similar resolution in 1904.[80]

8. Rules of the Senate.

Under the rules of the Senate as at present constituted it is possible for a minority to obstruct the passage of a measure by preventing a vote thereon. This may be done, and in the history of the Senate has been done frequently by continued debate, or what is termed fili-

[78]Ames, p. 66.
[79]App., No. 201.
[80]App., No. 408.

bustering. These prolonged debates have sometimes embarrassed the country by delaying the passage of other measures in addition to the one filibustered. On July 31, 1916, Senator Chilton, of West Virginia, introduced two amendments in the endeavor to change the Senate rules. One of them provided that after 10 days' debate on any certain bill or resolution, any Senator had the privilege to move for a vote on the measure, and that that motion would have precedence over any other business. This motion was to be debated not exceeding six hours on a side, limiting each Senator to 30 minutes, and the final discussion to be for at least 20 hours on a side.

The resolution ended with the statement that " It shall be the duty of the Presiding Officer of the Senate to enforce this rule without any request or point of order being made."[81] The other amendment provided that " No rule of the Senate shall prevent a majority of the Senate from amending its rules by a yea-and-nay vote taken after as much as 20 hours' debate upon each side of any proposed rule or amendment to a rule."[82]

In the nature of things it is hardly possible that an amendment of this nature would ever be accepted by the Senate. Under the Constitution (Art. I, sec. 5, cl. 2) it now has the right to make rules as drastic as it may choose. Exercising this right, in 1917 this body endeavored to control filibustering by promulgating a rule that (1) on petition of 16 Senators a motion to cut off discussion on any bill can be served on the House and (2) if adopted two days later by a two-thirds vote it will bring the debate to an end, after each Member has en-

[81]App., No. 849.
[82]App., No. 850.

joyed the right to speak for not more than one hour on the pending measure.[83]

The occasional abuse or alleged abuse of the immunity granted Representatives and Senators in Article I, section 6, of the Constitution has actuated one legislator to propose the addition to this section of the provision "that this provision shall not apply to any speech not actually spoken in debate on the floor of either House without reasonable justification and with the willful intent to injure the character of any person." [84]

On March 15, 1928, Mr. Golder, of Pennsylvania, introduced an amendment to take the place of the first paragraph of section 6 of Article I of the Constitution. This resolution repeats that section but omits that part which reads that "for any speech or debate in either House they shall not be questioned in any other place." [85]

[83] Beard, p. 275.
[84] App., No. 864.
[85] App., No. 1352.

CHAPTER II

PROPOSED AMENDMENTS AFFECTING THE FORM OF GOVERNMENT: EXECUTIVE

9. Changing date of Inauguration Day.

With the movement to change the time of the sessions of Congress, discussed in section 1, there has been coupled the agitation for a change in the date of Inauguration Day. In fact a good many of the amendments covering either subject include the other.

The many attempts made to change the date of Inauguration Day have been based mainly upon two reasons: First, to have the inaugural day come in a more favorable season of the year; second, to have the President's term fit logically into the plans for changing the beginning and ending dates of the Congress.

In 1876 a resolution was introduced in Congress endeavoring to change the date of Inauguration Day to May 1. In 1886 an attempt was made to change the date to April 30 so as to have it fall on the anniversary of Washington's first inauguration. In 1889 another amendment was introduced fixing the last Tuesday of April as Inaugural Day, this occurring on April 30 in that year, the object being to celebrate the one-hundredth anniversary of Washington's first inaugural to the day.[1]

Since 1889, 81 amendments have been presented in some form or other attempting to change the date of

[1]Ames, p. 36.

Inauguration Day; 18 have designated April 30 as the Inaugural Day;[2] 5 have designated the last Wednesday in April;[3] 14 the last Thursday in April;[4] 2 the first Tuesday in May;[5] 22 some day in the early part of January;[6] 19 in the latter part of January;[7] and 1 the second Monday in December.[8]

Although March 4 has generally proven itself a bad day for the ceremonials and pageants attendant upon the installation of the new President, the difficulty in changing the date has been in the inability of Congress to agree on any certain date in the spring as being more conducive to good weather than any other. In the consideration of Senate Resolution 83[9] on May 10, 1898, after Senator Hoar had spoken of the inclement and disagreeable weather of the preceding Inauguration Days, and had pleaded for the more agreeable date provided in his resolution, the last Wednesday in April, Senator Perkins, of California, showed by reports from the Weather Bureau that from 1873, when the Weather Bureau was established, to 1897, inclusive, the only advantage of the last Wednesday in April over March 4 seemed to be that on three of the April days there were high winds and threat-

[2] App., Nos. 5, 10, 23, 24, 31, 51, 80, 85, 97, 98, 125, 215, 240, 333, 376, 435, 553, 569.

[3] App., Nos. 285, 318, 340, 532, 582.

[4] App., Nos. 351, 368, 430, 431, 519, 521, 555, 556, 557, 567, 571, 613, 525, 686.

[5] App., Nos. 410, 520.

[6] App., Nos. 556a, 570, 692, 697, 766, 777, 792, 799, 826, 858, 896, 1029, 1309, 1317, 1318, 1323, 1328, 1333, 1340, 1344, 1351, 1362.

[7] App., Nos. 1044, 1052, 1129, 1136, 1146, 1170, 1171, 1181, 1189, 1208, 1209, 1215, 1234, 1259, 1272, 1278, 1284, 1288, 1289.

[8] App., No. 1027.

[9] App., No. 240.

ening weather in place of snow or sleet, the other days having matched up quite evenly on good and bad weather.[10]

Another objection to the last Wednesday in April, or any particular day of the week, is that it would cause a change from term to term in the exact number of days in the term. The Constitution states the President's term to be four years (Art. III, sec. 1), but as week days by name advance in date from year to year the term of one incumbent would be less than four years, while his successor's would be more than four years.[11] In answer to the contentions of the sponsors of the resolution that it would obviate the difficulties and inconveniences consequent upon March 4 falling upon Sunday, it was shown that in about 200 years it occurred on Sunday but six times,[12] this infrequency being ascribed to the peculiar results attendant upon Inauguration Day coming in the year following leap year.

There has been much discussion in Congress as to whether it is necessary to change the date of Inauguration Day by a constitutional amendment, the Constitution proper specifying no exact date for the inauguration.[13] Those in favor of the constitutional amendment maintain that since the President's term was fixed at four years by the Constitution an extension or curtailment of that period, which would be necessitated by a change in the

[10] Cong. Rec., May 10, 1898, p. 4763.

[11] Ibid., p. 4772.

[12] 1821, 1849, 1877, 1917, 1945, 1973.

[13] Ante, sec. 1. On Sept. 12, 1788, the Continental Congress declared the first Wednesday in Mar., 1789, to be the time for commencing proceedings under the new Constitution. This fell on Mar. 4. and that date has since been accepted as the official inaugural date.

inaugural date, could only constitutionally be effected by an amendment.

During recent years the resolutions seem tended toward having the President begin his term of office sometime in January, irrespective as to weather conditions. This is due probably to the fact that most of the gubernatorial inaugurations throughout the country occur in January, and also to the fact that in unusually severe weather the inaugural ceremony can be held in the Senate chamber, as was done on March 4, 1909, when Mr. Taft was inaugurated.

An interesting objection to having the inauguration occur in January was presented in the minority report opposing the passage of House Joint Resolution 93, Sixty-eighth Congress. This report declared that as the President, by reason of intensive campaigning, is subjected to a severe physical strain prior to the election, and as after the election he is compelled to severely exert himself in preparing his message to Congress, supervise a budget, plan governmental policies, select a cabinet, make speeches, and answer a great deal of correspondence personally concerning his election, it is dangerous for him to take up the burden of the presidential office but two months after the election, the present system, which permits four months' preparation, being more humane.[14]

The history of the resolutions on this subject indicate the impossibility of a constitutional amendment ever being adopted merely for the purpose of furnishing a pleasant day for inaugural ceremonies, there being much objection to "tinkering with the Constitution,"[15] for the

[14] 68th Cong., H. Rept. 211, pt. 2.

[15] Mr. English, of N. J., Cong. Rec., 52d Cong., 2d sess., p. 483.

purpose of "turning it into a weather vane."[16] It is probable, however, that in adjusting the congressional term, the subject discussed in section 1, the date of inauguration will be changed to better fit into the new plan finally chosen.

This was done in the last four resolutions on this subject which passed the Senate, a discussion of which follows.

Sixty-seventh Congress—Senate Joint Resolution 253

On November 22, 1922, Senator Caraway, of Arkansas, introduced a resolution (S. Con. Res. 29), the first one of its kind ever presented in Congress, declaring that "it is the sense of the Senate of the United States that all Members defeated at the recent polls abstain from voting on any but routine legislation, such as necessary supply bills, motions to adjourn, or motions to recess and such other legislation as does not involve any material change of policy." It was contended by Senator Caraway that legislators who were defeated at the polls in November, 1922, and who thus would not serve in the next Congress, could not have the proper feeling of responsibility toward their constituents and should not vote on matters of a permanent nature, and especially on questions raised in the preelection campaign.

This resolution was referred to the Committee on Agriculture and Forestry and reported back to the Senate on December 15, 1922, with the explanation that the passage of such a resolution "would interfere with the constitutional right and privilege of many Members of Congress." That under the Constitution "a Member's right, if not

[16] Cong. Rec., Mar. 16, 1900, p. 3264.

his duty, to participate fully in all legislation up to the close of his constitutional term can not be questioned." [17]

The report went on further, however, to say that the resolution showed " a very serious defect in some of the provisions of the Constitution," which defects should be remedied by means of a constitutional amendment providing for the convening of Congress and the inauguration of the President soon enough after elections to bring about legislation reflecting the opinions of the voters as expressed at the polls. Accordingly, an amendment was presented stipulating that the presidential term should begin the third Monday in January after the presidential election; that the President and Vice President should be elected directly by the people without the intervention of electors, although still retaining the electoral ratio among the States; that Senators and Representatives should take their oath of office on the first Monday in January following their election; that Congress should meet at least once a year on the first Monday in January, unless they chose by law a different date; and that the President, Senators, and Representatives in office upon the adoption of the amendment should relinquish their offices the third Monday and first Monday, respectively, in January preceding the March 4, which would otherwise mark the termination of their incumbencies.[18]

On February 12, 1923, when the resolution came before the Senate for debate, Senator Norris explained that since the time before the close of the session was short, and as there might be some opposition to the plan for the popular election of President, which would unduly delay and

[17] Cong. Rec., vol. 64, pt. 4, p. 3505.
[18] Ibid., pp. 3505–3537.

perhaps defeat the passage of the whole resolution, he had decided to omit that feature from the resolution. Accordingly, the debate was restricted to the remaining provisions of the resolution. The speeches covered generally the same arguments delivered on previous occasions on the same subject. The argument which was stressed more than any other was that one regarding the voting in Congress of legislators who had already been repudiated at the polls.[19]

The lack of opposition was remarkable, and when the amendment came to a vote on February 13 it was passed by a majority of 63 to 6.

On February 14 the resolution was referred to the House Committee on Election of President, Vice President, and Representatives in Congress.[20] Some minor changes were made, namely, that the presidential term should begin January 24 and the congressional term January 4; that Congress should meet at least once every year on January 4, and that in the event a President or Vice President is not selected before the time fixed for the beginning of the presidential term, Congress may declare who shall act as President until the House of Representatives chooses a President or the Senate chooses a Vice President.

[19] On this Senator Robinson, of Arkansas, said: "If it is desirable that the impulse and the impetuous demand for reform sometimes reflected in elections shall not be too promptly responded to, it is of even greater importance that when a question has been made an issue in a political campaign, when the voters have registered their decision and judgment affecting it, those who have been discredited and defeated shall not be permitted to defy the power which exalted them and override the will of the constituency by whose favor they enjoy public office." Ibid., p. 3494.

[20] Ibid., 3648.

The minority report filed to accompany this resolution objected to the amendment, declaring there was no necessity for an amendment; that the time of the sessions of Congress could be evened up by holding the congressional elections in October or even September and Congress could convene the first time in November or October. All this could be accomplished by legislation.[21]

On February 22, 1923, the amended resolution was put on the House Calendar,[22] a request was made for a special rule under which the resolution might be considered, but owing to the lateness of the session the chairman of the Committee on Rules declined to approve such a rule. The amendment thus died.

Sixty-eighth Congress—Senate Joint Resolution 22

At the commencement of the Sixty-eighth Congress Senator Norris, of Nebraska, introduced an amendment similar to the one just discussed, with an addition that if the House of Representatives, when the election of a President devolves upon it, has not by the third Monday in January elected a President, then the Vice President will serve as Acting President until the House of Representatives should choose a President. When the resolution came before the Senate for discussion, this latter proposition was very much objected to on the ground that it would make the President—that is, the Acting President—dependent entirely upon the House of Representatives and that body could oust him at any time it saw fit by choosing a President. To correct this, Senator Adams, of Colorado, then introduced an amendment to the resolution to the effect that when the Vice President takes

[21] 67th Cong., H. Rept. 1690, pt. 2.
[22] Cong. Rec., vol. 64, pt. 4, p. 4341.

office by reason of the inability of the House of Representatives to choose one, he should hold office " as in the case of the death or constitutional disability of the President." [23] The amendment was agreed to.

Senator McKellar, of Tennessee, then objected that the time between the date of the covening of Congress and the date of inauguration—that is, the first Monday and third Monday in January—was too short to assure election of a President.[24]

This apprehension was shared in by other Senators and it was deemed wise to extend the time for the House's deliberation until March 4, the time established by the twelfth amendment. This was agreed to.[25]

The debate on this resolution was somewhat extended by the introduction, by Senator Harris, of Georgia, of an amendment providing that the presidential term shall be six years with illegibility for reelection.[26] It was finally voted down, not so much on its individual merits, but because it was not germane to the pending resolution. As stated by Senator Pepper, of Pennsylvania, " the question involved in the amendment proposed by the Senator from Nebraska has to do merely with the mechanics of the government administration. The proposition involved in the amendment proposed by the Senator from Georgia has to do with a question fundamental in the structure and theory of our constitutional system." Further, that while the proposition advanced by Senator Harris was not unfamiliar to the Senate as an academic proposition it was relatively new as a matter of concrete proposition requir-

[23] Cong. Rec., vol. 65, pt. 5, Mar. 17, 1924, p. 4327.

[24] Ibid., p. 4328.

[25] Cong. Rec., vol. 65, pt. 4, p. 4412.

[26] Ibid., pp. 4141–4149.

ing action, and it had not been given the consideration which it deserves and should receive before affirmative action is taken upon it." This amendment to the resolution was defeated, 45 nays against 10 yeas.[27]

Speaking on the resolution itself, Senator Reed, of Missouri, opposed thereto, declared himself against the theory that good government requires immediate installation in office after election. On the contrary, he pointed out that an election during the congressional term, as is now the case, acts as a restraining influence on Congressmen and Senators and that a "body of men whose policies have been repudiated will be less likely to carry them out than they would if they had been sitting there before the election was held at all."[28]

An interesting point brought out by the Committee on the Judiciary recommending passage of the resolution was that when Senators were chosen by the legislatures it was difficult and sometimes impossible for Senators to be elected until February and March. Since the adoption of the seventeenth amendment, however, Senators have been elected by the people at the same time representatives were elected. "There is no reason, therefore," says the report, "why the Congress elected in November should not be sworn in and actually take up office at the beginning of the new year following the election."[29]

On March 18, 1924, the resolution was voted upon and passed, 63 yeas to 7 nays. On March 19, 1924, it was sent to the House Committee on Election of President, Vice President, and Representatives in Congress. From this committee it was reported back to the House on April 15

[27] Cong. Rec., vol. 65, pt. 4, p. 4326.

[28] Ibid., p. 4244.

[29] 68th Cong., S. Rept. No. 170, p. 6.

with amendments similar to those proposed to Senate Joint Resolution 253 of the previous Congress—namely, that Congress should meet the 4th day of January and the President should be inaugurated the 24th day of January. The committee proposed that there should be no limit to the time within which the House of Representatives shall choose a President, adding also that where the House of Representatives has not chosen a President before the time fixed for the beginning of his term and a Vice President has also not been chosen by the Senate, Congress may by law provide what officer shall act as President until the House of Representatives chooses a President or the Senate a Vice President.[30]

This amendment, or the resolution submitted by the Senate, did not come to a vote in the House of Representatives, and thus perished with the end of the Sixty-eighth Congress.

Sixty-ninth Congress—Senate Joint Resolution 9

On December 8, 1925, at the beginning of the first session of the Sixty-ninth Congress, Senator Norris once more introduced an amendment on this subject, this resolution particularly declaring that the presidential term shall begin the third Monday in January; the representative and senatorial terms to begin the first Monday in January, on which date Congress shall convene; further, if the House of Representatives does not choose a President before the beginning of the presidential term, the Vice President shall act as President until a President is chosen; if the House has not chosen a President before the following March 4, then the Vice President shall act as President during the remainder of the term; and Con-

[30] 68th Cong., House Calendar No. 147, Rept. No. 513.

gress shall provide by law who shall act as President in the event the Vice President is not chosen before the time fixed for the beginning of his term.[31]

This resolution was referred to the Committee on the Judiciary, which reported it back favorably, striking out the provision that if the President shall not be chosen before March 4 the Vice President shall act during the remainder of the term.[32]

With this amendment the resolution experienced little difficulty in the Senate, was debated very little, and passed the Senate on February 15, 1926, by a vote of 73 yeas to 2 nays.[33]

It was then sent to the House of Representatives, which referred it to the House Committee on Election of President, etc. This committee struck out the entire resolution after the resolving clause and inserted House Joint Resolution 164, which had already been reported favorably by the same committee on February 17, 1926.[34]

The House amendment provided that the presidential term shall commence January 24; the congressional term January 4; the Vice President to take office when the House of Representatives fails to choose one in time when the choice devolves upon it; and Congress to determine by law who shall act as President when neither President nor Vice President has been chosen in time.[35]

This amendment was never brought to a vote in the House and perished with the ending of the Sixty-ninth Congress.

---

[31] App., No. 1272.

[32] S. Rept. No. 12, 69th Cong.

[33] Cong. Rec., vol. 67, pt. 3, p. 3971.

[34] H. Rept. No. 311, 69th Cong.

[35] H. Rept. No. 362, 69th Cong.

Seventieth Congress—Senate Joint Resolution No. 47

At the beginning of the first session of the Seventieth Congress, Senator Norris, of Nebraska, introduced for the fourth time his constitutional amendment on the subject of presidential and congressional terms. It was referred to the Committee on Judiciary and reported back by that committee to the Senate on December 17, 1927.[36]

In answer to a question by Senator Fess, of Ohio, as to whether this resolution was similar to the one passed by the Senate on three previous occasions, Senator Norris replied:

> This is practically the same joint resolution that we have passed on three different occasions for three separate Congresses. The changes are immaterial. For instance, the last time the Senate passed the joint resolution, instead of providing that the term of the President and Vice President should begin, say, on the 2d day of January, it fixed the day of the week; and the same provision was made as to the beginning of the terms of the Members of Congress. On a previous occasion the joint resolution fixed the day of the month, as is done in the pending resolution. When the joint resolution was introduced at this session I changed it to its present form; but there is really no difference between the two. The only objection to this form is that the beginning of the term may come on Sunday, which is true under existing conditions. The House committee in reporting the resolution have reported it favorably every time it has been sent over there, but they have always insisted on putting in the day of the month rather than the day of the week. We thought to avoid any controversy with the House or with the House committee it would be just as well to change it in this instance.[37]

Senator Fess, speaking on the resolution, advanced the thought that there ought to be some provision made for a possible situation where the President and Vice Presi-

[36] H. Rept. No. 5, 70th Cong., 1st sess.
[37] Cong. Rec., Jan. 4, 1928, p. 952.

dent elect should die between the date when the electoral college meets and votes and submits its report and the date of the inauguration. In such a case there is no provision, either in the Constitution or in the law, that would provide for filling the vacancy.[38]

Senator Norris explained that his resolution did not cover that situation; neither did it cover another possible deficiency in the Constitution, namely—if it should occur that one or more of the candidates for President standing on the list of the three highest should die. "There is no way now under the Constitution by which that predicament could be met." [39]

With the exception of this discussion and a short speech by Senator Bingham, of Connecticut, doubting the wisdom of two long sessions, which this resolution might bring about, there was very little debate on the resolution, and on January 4, 1928, it passed the Senate by a vote of 67 yeas to 6 nays.[40]

The resolution was then referred to the House Committee on Election of President, etc. On March 6, 1928, Mr. Burton, of Ohio, reported that that committee, after considering Senate Joint Resolution No. 47, had approved of its purpose but had prepared a substitute resolution to submit to the House. This substitute constitutional amendment contained four sections, which provided:

First. That the terms of the President and Vice President should end on the 24th day of January and that of Senators and Representatives on the 4th day of January.

Second. That Congress should meet once a year—in the odd-numbered years on the 4th of January, and in the

---

[38] Cong. Rec., Jan. 4, 1928, p. 953.

[39] Ibid., p. 953.

[40] Ibid., p. 957.

even-numbered years it should also meet on the 4th of January, but the session should come to an end at noon on the 4th of May.

Third. That if the House of Representatives has not chosen a President whenever the right of choice devolves upon it, then the Vice President elect chosen for the ensuing term shall act as President until the House of Representatives chooses a President. (This section was included because of the contention that under the present Constitution there is some ambiguity whether the Vice President for the outgoing or the incoming term shall act as President in case of the failure of the House to choose a President before the beginning of the term.) The fourth section provided that if the President elect dies before the time fixed for the beginning of his term, then the Vice President elect shall become President. The amendment further authorized legislation by Congress to provide for the following contingencies:

(*a*) Where neither a President nor a Vice President has been chosen before the time fixed for the beginning of their terms.

(*b*) The death of both President and Vice President elect before the time fixed for the beginning of their terms.

(*c*) The death of any one of the three persons from whom the House of Representatives may choose a President whenever the right of choice devolves upon them.

(*d*) The death of either of the two persons from whom the Senate may choose a Vice President whenever the right of choice devolves upon them.[41]

Mr. Mapes, of Michigan, objected to Congress meeting 20 days before the inauguration of the President, declar-

[41] Cong. Rec., Mar. 6, 1928, p. 4194.

ing that except in such cases where the electoral college fails to elect a President there can be no advantage and there might be some embarrassment in having Congress wait around for 20 days doing nothing.[42] This same criticism was voiced by other Representatives.

Replying to this objection, Mr. Newton, of Minnesota, explained that Congress might transact all its investigating duties during the period in question.[42]

A great deal of opposition arose to the provision that in the even-numbered years Congress should adjourn on the 4th day of May. Mr. Celler, of New York, desired to know how, by having a fixed date set for adjournment, this could end the vice of filibuster. To this Mr. Burton replied that there would be four months, instead of three months, in which to legislate.[42]

During the discussion of the resolution, Mr. Bankhead, of Alabama, presented an argument on the advantages of a 4-year Representative term instead of a 2-year term.[43]

Mr. White, of Kansas, arguing for the adoption of the resolution, stated that under the present rule little is accomplished until after the 1st of January, so that during the short session there is only practically two months devoted to legislative activity, whereas under the proposed resolution there would be four months of sustained effort, and that in a session of four months the likelihood of a filibuster would be practically eliminated.[44]

Mr. Jeffers, of Alabama, was of the opinion that too many details were embodied in the resolution and that the constitutional amendment should merely contain the general idea of the change, leaving it to Congress to work

[42] Cong. Rec., Mar. 6, 1928, p. 4196.

[43] Ibid., p. 4197.

[44] Ibid., p. 4199.

out with suitable legislation the various points involved. He objected to the inclusion of specific dates, maintaining that a "flexible clause could be put into a constitutional amendment providing that the first Congress after the constitutional amendment should be ratified should enact the necessary legislation to set the date for the convening of Congress.[47]

Many of the arguments used in previous discussions on the advisability of having Representatives and Senators wait 13 months after election before taking office were repeated and there was much said about the so-called cooling-off period.

In arguing the merits of section 4 of the resolution under discussion, Mr. Lozier pointed out that if Coolidge had died between the second Monday of January, 1925, when the electoral college functioned, and the second Monday in February, the day the House of Representatives would have been called on to choose a President, the Republican Party would have been disfranchised because the present Constitution limits the choice to the highest three and the death of Mr. Coolidge would have left no Republican in this list of three. If John W. Davis had died in the period mentioned, the Democratic Party could not have elected a President.[48]

Mr. Merritt, of Connecticut, said, answering those who claimed that the 13-month delay was very injurious to the country, that "there is not the slightest fear that general public opinion which persists will not be duly embodied in the law." [49]

[47] Cong. Rec., Mar. 6, 1928, p. 4201.

[48] Ibid., p. 4206.

[49] Ibid., p. 4211.

Mr. Moore, of Virginia, explained that if Congress wishes to do it, it can provide for a new Congress to come in on the 4th of March, which will only mean a difference in time as provided in the proposed amendment between the date in January and the 4th of March.[50]

Mr. Temple, of Pennsylvania, opposing the resolution, declared that in case an election fails to result in the choice of a President through the electoral college, it would mean that the election was very close, in which event many congressional seats would be in dispute and it would be unwise to have such a disputed Congress decide a presidential contest.[51]

Mr. Newton favored the passage of the resolution but opposed the argument being used regarding the so-called " lame-duck " session, maintaining that " some of the best legislation that has passed Congress was passed during the hold-over session." He opposed the thought that the short session of Congress was " dominated by men who had been defeated at the polls and who, having been defeated, were striving to get even by enacting legislation that could not otherwise be passed." [52]

Mr. Montague, of Virginia, objected that under the proposed resolution there would not be time enough between November and January for the President to select his Cabinet officers, prepare his message, formulate his policies, and familiarize himself with the operation of the Government, especially the Budget system. Mr. Newton, of Minnesota, replying to this, said that the presidential nominee would have well-defined governmental ideas at the time of his nomination, and that if he did not, he

[50] Cong. Rec., Mar. 6, 1928, p. 4211.

[51] Ibid., p. 4214.

[52] Ibid., p. 4215.

would certainly formulate them in the course of his campaign.[53]

Mr. Luce, of Massachusetts, answering those who objected to the May 4 limitation, said that "it is but necessary for the President to call us together on the next day, without any of the task of organizing, electing the speaker, and choosing committees."[54]

Mr. Bankhead offered an amendment to the resolution that the "House of Representatives shall be composed of Members chosen every fourth year by the people of the several States."[55]

Mr. Ramseyer, of Iowa, made a point of order that this amendment was not germane to the resolution before the House. After debate on the point of order, the chairman of the Committee of the Whole (Mr. Lehlbach, of New Jersey) ruled that the proposed amendment was not germane. Mr. Bankhead appealed from the decision of the chair, but the decision was upheld on a vote of 207 ayes to 33 noes.[56]

Mr. Tucker, of Virginia, offered an amendment that if passed by Congress the resolution should be ratified by conventions in three-fourths of the States. This amendment was debated, voted on, and defeated by 90 ayes to 107 noes.[57]

Mr. Byrns, of Tennessee, reflected the opinion of many in favor of the resolution when he said that if the House eliminated the provision requiring the session in even-numbered years to be adjourned on May 4 he would vote

[53] Cong. Rec., Mar. 6, 1928, p. 4216.

[54] Cong. Rec., Mar. 8, 1928, p. 4354.

[55] Ibid., p. 4365.

[56] Ibid., p. 4370.

[57] Cong. Rec., Mar. 9, 1928, p. 4413.

for the resolution; otherwise he would have to vote against it.[58]

A motion by Mr. Chindblom, of Illinois, to strike out section 1 of the resolution, which if passed would defeat the main purpose of the resolution, was voted down.[59]

Mr. Jeffers, of Alabama, proposed an amendment that Congress should meet on the 4th day of January unless they should by law appoint a different day. The purpose of this amendment was to avoid the provision in the proposed resolution which required Congress to adjourn on May 4, and thus take away from the President the power whether or not to call Congress into session after May 4.

Mr. Mapes, of Michigan, offered an amendment to this amendment so that instead of January 4, the amendment would read the first Monday after the 4th of January. This would avoid the possibility of Congress having to meet on a Sunday.[60]

Mr. Garrett, objecting to the May 4 limitation, pointed out that if Congress were called upon to exercise its power of impeachment, it could not do so after this date. He said:

> With a limitation such as this proposed fixed by the Constitution itself, Congress might be helpless even in the exigency of an impeachment of the Executive himself. After May 4 the President is the only power that can bring the Congress back together under this proposition.[61]

A vote was taken on an amendment proposed by Mr. Simmons, of Nebraska, and modified by Mr. Mapes so that the resolution would read that Congress, instead of

---

58 Cong. Rec., Mar. 9, 1928, p. 4414.

59 Ibid., p. 4415.

60 Ibid., p. 4420.

61 Ibid., p. 4421.

meeting on the 4th day of January, would meet on the first Monday after January 4. This was rejected by 38 ayes to 96 noes.[62]

In considering section 3 of the resolution, Mr. Leavitt, of Montana, suggested that the situation outlined in that section had not been sufficiently studied to permit of a constitutional amendment, and along that line he had proposed a bill (H. R. 11853) providing for the appointment of a joint committee of the House and Senate to consider the electoral question. That joint committee would be composed of three Members of the House and three Members of the Senate Judiciary Committees, all lawyers. It would be their duty to take into consideration all circumstances involved in the present electoral situation and propose to Congress "a sound amendment to meet the needs of the situation." [63]

Mr. Lea, of California, offered an amendment to section 3 to provide for vacancies "in every case which may occur before the President is installed in his office." The present resolution, he pointed out, failed to provide for the case of inability, "which includes both mental and physical inability." This amendment was agreed to.[64]

Mr. Garrett, of Tennessee, proposed that the resolution should carry a clause that it be inoperative unless ratified within seven years by three-fourths of the legislatures, the entire membership of at least one branch of which should have been elected subsequent to the date of submission. This amendment carried on a vote of 187 ayes against 23 noes.[65]

---

[62] Cong. Rec., Mar. 9, 1928, p. 4423.

[63] Ibid., p. 4423.

[64] Ibid., p. 4425.

[65] Ibid., p. 4429.

Mr. La Guardia, of New York, moved that the resolution be separated. The chairman ruled that the "whole proposition is so nearly one single substantive proposition" that a clear-cut division could not be made and he so held, which decision was sustained by the House sitting as a Committee on the Whole.[66]

Upon termination of the debate the House accepted the whole House amendment to Senate Joint Resolution 47.

The completed resolution was then put to a vote and the result was 209 yeas and 157 nays. Two-thirds of the House having failed to vote in favor thereof, the joint resolution was accordingly rejected.[67]

10. Presidential electors.

During the period prior to the agitation for election of the President by popular vote, many amendments were submitted designed to improve upon the electoral system. The most frequent amendment introduced in this respect was that requiring the States to choose the presidential electors by designated districts, either using the congressional district as a working basis with the two extra electors to be selected in some other way, or redistricting the State according to the number of electors to be chosen. Forty-three amendments of this character have been introduced, a large proportion of them belonging to the period between 1800 and 1826.[68]

During the first 40 years of the Republic, three different systems of choosing electors were used: Election by the State legislature, election by the people by districts, and election by the people by general ticket. The Con-

[66] Cong. Rec., Mar. 9, 1928, p. 4428.

[67] Ibid., p. 4430.

[68] Ames, p. 84. App., No. 728.

stitution (Art. II, sec. 1) permits each State to appoint its presidential electors as it sees fit, and thus nothing short of a constitutional amendment would be required to compel a uniform method of choosing electors throughout the country. By 1832, however, all States, with the exception of South Carolina, of their own volition, put into effect the principal system of electing electors by general ticket[69] and thus the amendment became unnecessary, although an amendment on the subject was introduced in 1892.[70]

An amendment proposed in 1912[71] was designed to enlarge the freedom of the States in choosing presidential electors, rendering ineffective the present constitutional provision permitting Congress to determine the time of choosing the electors. (Art. II, sec. 1, cl. 3.)

The last resolution touching this subject was presented in 1913 by Mr. Murray, of Oklahoma. It provided that the number of electors should be equal to the number of Representatives in Congress and that they should be elected by congressional district. No provision was made for the election of the two State electors represented by the Senators of the State, so it is assumed that to that extent Mr. Murray intended to reduce the electoral vote of each State.[72]

11. Election of President and Vice President by a general direct vote; also general electoral vote.

On January 4, 1826, Mr. McManus, of New York, introduced an amendment providing for the direct election of the President and Vice President by the people with-

[69] Putney, A. H., Handbook on Election Laws, pp. 251–252.
[70] App., No. 105.
[71] App., No. 641.
[72] App., No. 728.

out the intervention of electors.[73] This action was doubtlessly induced by the result of the election of 1824, when Andrew Jackson, although receiving the largest popular vote, was defeated in the House of Representatives.[74] From 1826 to 1889 the same proposition in various forms was presented some thirty-four times.[75]

The frequency with which this amendment is introduced in Congress is due to the much-discussed belief that the presidential elector is entirely unnecessary, for, contrary to the instrument which created him, he acts merely as ordered and not as his own judgment dictates.[76] It also happens occasionally that the electoral vote of a State may not be an exact reflection of that State's opinion on the Presidency, as, for instance, when an elector is voted for merely on his own popularity, or voted against on his unpopularity, entirely aside from his party connection, in which event votes may go for or against a presidential candidate on issues for which he is not responsible.[77] It can also be well assumed that "some ballots are lost through failure to mark, for support or rejection, some names of electoral candidates upon 'blanket ballots' containing scores, or maybe hundreds, of names of electoral aspirants for an empty office." [78]

Under the electoral system as at present constituted it is possible for a President to be elected, although receiving less popular votes than his opponent, as was true with

[73] Ames, p. 88.

[74] Stanwood, History of Presidential Elections, p. 88.

[75] Ames, p. 88.

[76] Dougherty, J. H. The Electoral System of the United States, p. 250.

[77] H. Rept. No. 2439, 52d Cong., 2d sess.

[78] H. Rept. No. 2439, 52d Cong., 2d sess.

Hayes and Harrison in 1876 and 1888, respectively.[79] This, however, is not necessarily a defect which subverts the will of the Nation because the intention of the framers of the Constitution was that the President should be elected on a basis of State representation rather than by the compounded will of the masses. (This is exemplified by the fact that the States may appoint the electors as they choose, Art. II, sec. 2, Const., and that the number of electors is equal to the number of Senators and Representatives to which the State is entitled in Congress, thus allowing the small States, through the electoral vote corresponding to the two Senators, a voting strength much in excess of the popular vote.) This principle is carried out by many of the proposed amendments providing for the direct vote, as will be observed later.

From 1889 to 1928, 53 attempts have been made to change the present method of electing Presidents. These amendments group themselves into three classes: Those providing for a direct plurality vote, those providing for the electoral ratio, and those having a combination of both.

From the Fifty-first to the Fifty-fourth Congress, inclusive, 15 amendments for altering the method of choosing the President were proposed. It appears that at this time there was as yet no great demand for an abolition of the State lines, and the compounding into one mass of the American people, for the purpose of electing a President, for 11 of these amendments specifically retained the State electoral ratio based upon the combined number of Representatives and Senators in Congress.[80]

[79] Stanwood, E. History of Presidential Elections, pp. 138, 331.
[80] App., Nos. 17, 28, 92, 100, 103, 106, 109, 111, 113, 122, 128.

For the rest of the period (1906 to 1928), however, this idea of electoral representation appears eight times.[81] These amendments also provide that if no candidate receive a majority of the electoral vote the House of Representatives should determine from the candidates receiving the three highest numbers the successful candidate. An amendment introduced in 1924 by Senator Johnson, of California, provides that a plurality of the electoral votes shall be sufficient to elect a President and Vice President.[82]

A similar amendment was introduced by Mr. Lea, of California, in January, 1928.[83]

Of the methods other than that of the electoral ratio, 19 amendments provided simply that in a general election to be held on the same day throughout the country, the one receiving the highest number of votes should be elected President.[84]

Many others also provided for the direct plural vote, but included various features of balloting. Senator Peffer, of Kansas, proposed two amendments in the Fifty-second and Fifty-third Congresses designed to insure a majority vote for the candidate receiving the highest number of votes. This was to be effected by printing on the ballots this instruction to the officers of election:

> This ballot shall be first counted for the person named therein for President and Vice President, and if such person fails to receive within the United States the highest number of votes for the office for which he is designated upon ballots having a like caption, then this ballot shall be counted for the person having said highest number of votes.[85]

---

[81]App., Nos. 823, 858, 896, 1092, 1136, 1170, 1192, 1309.

[82]App., No. 1252.

[83]App., No. 1346.

[84]App., Nos. 135, 435, 656, 694, 697, 800, 814, 835, 854, 855, 856, 883.

[85]App. Nos. 83. 135

This sort of a preferential ballot would obviate the need of a second election, as provided for in the amendment introduced by Mr. Hobson, of Alabama, five times in two years (1911–1913),[86] and five more times by others.[87] This amendment declared also that if no candidate received a majority of the votes cast, then a second election should be called with the two candidates receiving the highest numbers as opponents.

Sixteen of the amendments included provisions for the direct nomination of the President by the people through primaries.[88]

Three amendments introduced in 1913 provide that if the electoral votes are tied between contending candidates then the one getting the most popular votes shall be declared elected.[89]

One amendment proposed to assign 1 electoral vote to each Congressional district in the country, and the carrying of a majority of these congressional districts was to constitute election.[90]

The balance of the amendments designated no particular plan for the election of the President other than he should be elected by a direct vote, leaving it to Congress to work out the necessary details.[91]

SUMMARY ON DIRECT ELECTION OF PRESIDENT

The great number of resolutions attempting to alter Amendment XII of the Constitution would indicate that

[86]App., Nos. 620, 665, 678, 680, 681.

[87]App., Nos. 84, 651, 766, 853, 943.

[88]App., Nos. 620, 651, 665, 678, 680, 681, 703, 711, 714, 755, 834, 1133, 1136, 1162, 1170, 1239.

[89]App., Nos. 703, 711, 714.

[90]App., No. 766.

[91]App., Nos. 162, 666, 700, 834, 857.

at some time in the near future the electoral college may be abolished. It is not probable, however, that the electoral vote will be discontinued. An amendment providing for the popular election of the President with a complete disregarding of State lines would hardly be ratified by the requisite three-fourths of the States.

On the other hand, there should not be any difficulty in securing the ratification of an amendment which would preserve the electoral strength of each State based upon the congressional representation. The voter in each State would thereby vote directly for the President and thus obviate the chance of splitting the vote of a State, as sometimes happens.[92]

On October 5, 1917, the Senate Committee on Judiciary reported such a resolution with the recommendation that it do not pass.[93]

Two of the five resolutions for direct election of the President introduced by Mr. DeArmond, of Missouri, provided for minority representation in the State by dividing the electoral vote of each State in proportion to the number of popular votes cast in the State for the several candidates for President and Vice President. This system also provided that the electoral vote should be exact, so that instead of giving the odd vote to the person having the highest number of votes in the State it would be divided in fractions among the contestants according to the popular vote, the fractions to be expressed in decimals not

[92] S. Rept. No. 165, 65th Cong., 1st sess. Since 1872, 13 States have split their vote under the present system. California split in 1912; West Virginia split in 1916.

[93] S. Rept. No. 165, pt. 2, 65th Cong., 1st sess.

exceeding four in number. A House report on this proposition declared that—

> It will be found upon investigation that if whole votes be given those having the largest fraction of the popular vote, the election may depend upon these fractions, thus making the electoral votes obtained on fractions the controlling votes in a close contest, thereby perpetuating though mitigating, perhaps, evils of which minority representation is thought to afford a remedy.[94]

12. Term of the President and Vice President.

Although no provision is made in the Constitution as to the number of terms the same person may be elected President it has become the " unwritten law " of the land set by Washington's precedent that a longer tenure than two terms involves a risk to our republican institutions.[95] It has been assumed by many of our legislators that this " unwritten law " is not a sufficient guaranty against undue continuity in office, and that it is possible for a very popular President to be elected a third time and even more. The efforts to elect Grant and Roosevelt for third terms lend weight to this contention. Accordingly many amendments designed to prohibit a longer tenure than two terms have been proposed to the Constitution. Many other amendments have attempted to restrict the President's incumbency to one term. A third class of amendments also provided for restricting the President to one term but lengthening the term.

Over 125 amendments were introduced during the first 100 years of the Nation's history embracing one or more

[94] H. Rept. No. 2439, 52d Cong., 2d sess.

[95] Bryce. The American Commonwealth, i, 42.

of these principles.[96] Since 1889, 85 proposals with the same objects in view have been advanced. The peaks of these amendments came in the 2-year periods of 1892–93 and 1912–13, undoubtedly suggested by the unusual occurrence in American history of an ex-President running for election after an absence of four years from office, and another ex-President seeking a third term also after an intervening term of absence. In the first period (1892–93) 14 of these amendments were submitted. Seven provided for a 6-year term with no reeligibility to a second term,[97] four were designed to prevent a President from succeeding himself in office,[98] two made two consecutive terms of office the limit,[99] and one made one term the limit.[1] During the Rooseveltian period (1912–13) 22 proposals for these constitutional amendments were advanced. Fifteen set six years for the President's term with ineligibility for a second term,[2] three prohibited a third term,[3] two provided for a single 7-year term,[4] and one prohibited any more than two consecutive terms in office.[5]

It will be observed that the great number of amendments introduced during these 2-year periods did not necessarily indicate a censure of Mr. Cleveland's and Mr. Roosevelt's efforts for reelection, but only manifested the

[96] Ames, p. 123.

[97] App., Nos. 64, 72, 92, 95, 107, 109, 122.

[98] App., Nos. 99, 111, 113, 128.

[99] App., Nos. 83, 135.

[1] App., No. 134.

[2] App., Nos. 631, 633, 641, 642, 645, 657, 669, 693, 697, 700, 710, 711, 716, 718, 720.

[3] App., Nos. 632, 661, 695.

[4] App., Nos. 665, 681.

[5] App., No. 703.

need for a definite constitutional statement as to the most desirable length of presidential term and whether succession in office was or was not dangerous to the best interests of the country.

On February 21, 1927, Mr. Fairchild, of New York, presented a resolution providing that no person shall be elected President "who has previously served two terms whether by election or by succession due to the removal, death, resignation, or inability of the President, where the term by succession shall have continued for a period of two years or more."[6] This amendment was undoubtedly designed to settle the question, which was so much discussed before President Coolidge withdrew from the nominational race, as to whether the unexpired term served by an ascending Vice President should be considered a term in the calculation of the "2-term rule."

On December 21, 1927, Senator Dill, of Washington, submitted a resolution declaring that no person shall serve as President more than eight years, without specifying whether the eight years shall be composed of successive terms.[7]

13. Presidential self-succession.

The biggest objection voiced against succession in office is that the President can so distribute the patronage so as to insure his renomination and greatly assist his reelection. This has been declared dangerous in two ways: First, in that it imperils the republican institutions to have one man with such a powerful political machine in his control, and second, that it greatly interferes with the efficiency of the Government's work through its departments.

[6] App., No. 1305.
[7] App., No. 1339.

The direct applicability of presidential self-succession to Government efficiency was attempted to be shown through the referring of Senate Resolution 62 in the Fifty-second Congress to the Senate Committee on Civil Service and Retrenchment, instead of to the Committee on the Judiciary, which usually considers constitutional amendments. This amendment, introduced by Senator Stewart, of Nevada, provided that " no person who has held the office of President for a term of four years or any part thereof shall be eligible to that office within four years after the expiration of such term."[8] Since the Committee on Civil Service and Retrenchment had charge of matters pertaining to the preventing of political influence operating upon appointments, it was contended by the authors of the resolution that this committee should consider the resolution for, " if it be important the clerks and minor officials should be removed from political influence in their appointment, it is of much more importance that the executive head, who exercises the power and patronage of the whole Government, should be relieved from all temptation to use the power in his hands to reelect himself to that office."[9]

The tendency toward limiting the President to one term is criticized by the supporters of the plan under discussion on the ground that the arguments which recommend the prevention of a President succeeding himself do not justify his perpetual exclusion from office. Grover Cleveland is the only instance of a President leaving office and later being reelected, and " there is nothing in this solitary

[8] App., No. 99.

[9] Cong. Rec., Mar. 11, 1892, p. 1901.

instance to suggest the policy of unending ineligibility to reelection." [10]

During the last 39 years six amendments have been proposed to make self-succession in the presidential office impossible.[11] Four resolutions have been submitted prohibiting more than two successive terms.[12] One amendment introduced in 1920 declared that no President shall serve more than two terms, without designating whether it means two successive terms or two terms in all.[13]

14. One-term Presidency.

This section will be devoted to those amendments which call for a single-term Presidency without designating the number of years, thus continuing the 4-year term. The 6-year single-term amendments will be discussed in the succeeding section.

In accepting the Democratic presidential nomination in 1884, Mr. Cleveland said: [14]

> When we consider the patronage of this great office, the allurements of power, the temptation to retain public office once gained, and, more than all, the availability a party finds in an incumbent, whom a horde of officeholders, with a zeal borne of benefits received and fostered by the hope of favors yet to come, stand ready to aid, with money and trained political assistants, we recognize in the eligibility of the President for reelection the most serious danger to that calm, deliberate, and intelligent action which must characterize a government by the people.

---

[10] H. Rept. No. 2439, 52d Cong., 2d sess.

[11] App., Nos. 50, 99, 111, 113, 128, 156.

[12] App., Nos. 83, 135, 703, 918.

[13] App., No. 1020.

[14] Addresses, State Papers and Letters of Grover Cleveland, p. 52. Ed. Elbert Bergh.

Mr. Hayes in his acceptance speech in 1876 also affirmed "that the restoration of the civil service to the system established by Washington and followed by the early Presidents can best be accomplished by an executive who is under no temptation to use the patronage of his office to promote his own reelection." [15]

The Democratic platform of 1912 pledged itself to the observance of the single-term principle.[16] These declarations in favor of the single-term policy were naturally reflected in the proposed amendments to the Constitution. In 1894 Mr. Bryan, of Nebraska, introduced three amendments providing for a single-term presidency,[17] and another one making a President ineligible to succeed himself.[18] In 1889, 1893, 1908, 1909, and 1912, five other amendments were submitted with the single-term provision.[19]

Those opposed to the single-term idea claim that there is nothing in the history of the United States to show that 2-term Presidents are dangerous. In a speech on this subject, Senator Borah, of Idaho, enumerated the Presidents that had served two terms, and added:

> No line of rulers or chief magistrates, whether of hereditary sovereigns coming down through successive generations or the freely chosen of a free people, can compare with this line of remarkable Presidents.[20]

Woodrow Wilson says on this subject: [21]

> Efficiency is the only just foundation for confidence in a public officer, under republican institutions no less than under monarchs,

[15] National Republican Nomination, Library of Congress, E680, H41, p. 2.

[16] Stanwood, Edward. A History of the Presidency, p. 272.

[17] App., Nos. 153, 154, 155.

[18] App., No. 156.

[19] App., Nos. 4, 134, 498, 525, 630.

[20] Cong. Rec., Aug. 20, 1912, p. 11361.

[21] Wilson, Woodrow. Congressional Government, p. 255.

and short terms which cut off the efficient as surely and as inexorably as the inefficient are quite as repugnant to republican as to monarchical rules of wisdom.

It is also pointed out by opponents to the 1-term idea that it frequently happens a President's first term approaches its end in the midst of a national crisis, and it would be unwise to deprive the country of the services of the man most familiar with the responsibilities and needs of the day and thus more able to guide the Nation through its crisis.[22]

15. Six-year presidential term.

A 6-year term with no reeligibility to a second term, in point of times introduced, seems to be the most favored of the plans advanced. During the last 39 years it has been proposed no less than sixty-three times,[23] and on February 1, 1913, one of the resolutions (S. J. Res. 78) passed the Senate by a vote of 47 yeas to 23 nays.[24] It was referred to the House Committee on Judiciary, but was not reported to the House before the end of the session.[25]

---

[22] There are some who believe also that a third term is not inconsistent with governmental efficiency, and that the precedent established by Washington should not morally bind his successors to a 2-term limit. His reasons for refusing a third term were more personal than patriotic, as his physical condition had made it almost impossible for him to continue in office.—Third Term, by Timothy O. How, North American Review, February, 1880.

[23] App., Nos. 21, 28, 38, 64, 72, 92, 95, 107, 109, 122, 141, 162, 203, 243, 255, 281, 308, 392, 409, 410, 435, 447, 448, 485, 487, 493, 494, 514, 522, 531, 617, 613, 633, 641, 642, 645, 657, 669, 681, 697, 700, 710, 711, 716, 718, 720, 766, 777, 792, 801, 826, 827, 835, 846, 858, 923, 1021, 1079, 1096, 1133, 1177, 1239, 1331.

[24] Cong. Rec., 63d Cong., 3d sess., p. 2419.

[25] Cong. Rec., 63d Cong., 3d sess. (App.), 633.

The 6-year term is intended as a sort of compromise between the single 4-year term and the double 4-year term with all the declared advantages of less frequent elections and the abolishment of alleged patronage schemes to insure reelections. In the consideration of the above-mentioned resolution (S. J. Res. 78), Senator Cummins, of Iowa, declared that if there was anything in the writings of the framers of the Constitution which conflicted with the idea of a 6-year presidential term, that should not be an obstacle to the change because the country has changed considerably since the Constitution was created. The President of the United States now has more power than any other executive in the world, appointing, as he does, practically the entire civil and military staff of the Government; being commander in chief of the land and naval forces; and treating directly with foreign countries. While these powers are all enumerated in the Constitution, yet they have taken on a great deal more importance and responsibilities since Washington's time.[26] For this reason Senator Cummins urged that the President "should be free from the temptation of ambition as he should be free from the coercion of influences that always surround one invested with great power." "The single term would wipe out all these influences seeking preferment as compensation for assistance rendered in electing the President to a second term."[27]

Senator Borah, who was opposed to the resolution, said that the 6-year term was undesirable because if the incumbent is pursuing a course detrimental to the Nation's welfare this will continue him in office for two more years,

---

[26] Hill, John P. The Federal Executive, pp. 1–12.

[27] Cong. Rec., Aug. 19, 1912, p. 11255.

and if he is a wise President and his services are invaluable to the country this resolution makes his continuance in the service impossible.[28]

The debate on this resolution started on March 11, 1912, and continued to February 1, 1913, going through the periods of the presidential nominations and elections of 1912 when party fever ran high and candidates were warmly defended and attacked by their respective friends and enemies in the Senate. The question arose as to whether President Taft and ex-President Roosevelt should be exempted from the provisions of the amendment should it go into effect. On January 30, 1913, Senator Clarke, of Arkansas, introduced an amendment to the constitutional amendment so as exclude these two persons from its workings.[29] Senator Root, of New York, contended that changing the Constitution was too serious and important a matter to be complicated by any personal consideration, and that the proposed amendment should apply to all, including President-elect Wilson, if it should be adopted in time.[30] Senator Lodge, of Massachusetts, was also opposed to the exclusion of Roosevelt, Taft, and Wilson, stating that if an exemption were made in their favor, they might occupy a most anomalous position in the Republic by holding office respectively for 13, 10, and 10 years, should they be reelected to office.[31] This amendment was defeated. Other amendments to make the term a single one of four years, as at present constituted, to include a provision for the direct vote of the President, and to make two terms of four years each the limit, were

[28] Cong. Rec., Aug. 20, 1912, p. 11355.
[29] Cong. Rec., Jan. 30, 1913, p. 2264.
[30] Ibid., p. 2265.
[31] Ibid., p. 2348.

all rejected. An amendment was introduced by Senator Bristow, of Kansas, to give Congress power to provide for the recall of the President by a popular vote at any biennial election, claiming that if the President did not carry out the policies for which he stood when elected, the people should have the right to recall him. This amendment was defeated.[32] After amendments the resolution itself read:

> The term of office of President shall be six years, and no person who has held the office by election and discharged its power or duties or acted as President under the Constitution and laws made in pursuance thereof shall be eligible to hold again the office by election.

This was passed by a vote of 42 yeas to 23 nays.[33] It never reached the House.

16. Settlement of contested presidential elections.

The difficulties and national embarrassment experienced in the election of a President by the House of Representatives when the electoral college fails of a choice has led to the introduction of many resolutions calculated to obviate delay and uncertainty in this matter. Some of these have provided that the Supreme Court shall decide contested elections; some that a second election shall be held; others that Congress should be given power to elect by joint ballot; and still others that a tribunal of some kind should be constituted to act in contested cases.[34]

The last-mentioned method was urged upon Congress twice in 1892 and once in 1893 by Mr. De Armond, of Missouri.[35] In an able report on House Joint Resolution

[32] Cong. Rec., Jan. 30, 1913, p. 2273.

[33] Cong. Rec., Feb. 1, 1913, p. 2419.

[34] Ames, pp. 116–122.

[35] App., Nos. 111, 113, 128.

No. 200, introduced in the Fifty-second Congress, he indicated that while Congress should primarily decide simple differences in the presidential election contests, a higher court or court of last resort should be in existence for the conclusive decision, should there be any great doubt as to the returns. This court, he stated, "ought to be so constituted, if possible, as to command the unquestioning respect and confidence of the country. That degree of respect and confidence can not be secured for any tribunal unless it be thought to possess the highest qualifications of ability and learning supported by the greatest freedom from partiality." He added further that the committee reporting the resolution "do not draw sufficient encouragement from the history of our country to lead us to look upon our national legislature, or either house thereof, as such a tribunal."[36]

His resolution provided that the tribunal should consist of the Chief Justice of the United States and the chief justices of the highest court of each State, or a majority of them, as some might be interested in the contest or unable or unwilling to sit. The court would have complete jurisdiction to decide all issues raised in the contest and determine not only the legal returns but have power also to go behind them in the judicial determination of choosing the properly elected candidate for President or Vice President.

This tribunal which would be called the Court of Chief Justices would be called into action when either House of Congress declared that the result of a presidential election depended upon the vote of any specified State or States, and "that it ought to be judicially determined for whom of right such vote or votes should be counted." It was

[36] H. Rept. No. 2439, 52d Cong., 2d sess.

probably the reluctance to enforce upon the judges of the respective States a Federal duty, and thus come into conflict with the State rights doctrine that caused the omission of any mandatory provision for the operations of the State chief justices in this contemplated tribunal. As, therefore, it might be possible that enough would refuse to appear to constitute the court, the resolution provided that in the event the court did not convene, or convening could not come to a decision at least five days before the date of inauguration, then in that event the congressional count should be final.[37] This resolution was never voted upon.

A study of the mechanism of the Constitution and of constitutional history makes it plain that numerous intricate questions are possible in the application of constitutional provisions to the exigencies of public events. To resolve these questions before they arise, and thus save the Government embarrassment, was evidently the purpose of Senator Fess and Representative Cable, both of Ohio, when they introduced in their respective Houses a resolution providing that a constitutional amendment commission be appointed by the President, House, and Senate, to study the questions outlined therein (given here in footnote)[38] and report thereon.

---

[37] H. Rept. No. 2439, 52d Cong., 2d sess.

[38] App., Nos. 1249, 1250. The text of the resolutions is as follows:

"Whereas the provisions for the election and terms of President and Vice President, and the terms of Senators and Representatives require comprehensive amendments to the Constitution; and

"Whereas under the present method the following questions having arisen which have not been finally determined or perfected by proper amendment or legislation, to wit:

"(a) Does the Secretary of State succeed to the Presidency if for any reason there is no constitutionally elected President by March 4?

On May 29, 1928, Mr. Browne, of Wisconsin, proposed an amendment to the Constitution providing that when the choice of President devolves upon the House of Repre-

---

"(b) Shall there be a special election? Or does the person succeeding to the presidency fill out the unexpired term?

"(c) If the election were ordered in case of a vacancy in the office, could it be for the unexpired term or would it have to be for a term of four years, thus disarranging the four-year period of the Government?

"(d) Does the commission of a Cabinet officer expire on March 4, and would this prevent succession?

"(e) For what length of time would a Cabinet officer act as President?

"(f) Shall the choice of a Chief Executive be intrusted to the House of Representatives about to go out of existence when such House may even be under control of the party defeated at the preceding November election?

"(g) Where the President elect dies before the second Wednesday in February, may the House of Representatives elect a President?

"(h) In case of failure to count the votes and declare the results by the 4th of March, where the electors have not failed to elect but Congress has failed to declare the result, may the count continue?

"(i) Would the Vice President elect succeed to the presidency should the President elect die before the 4th of March?

"(j) Who would be President in case both President elect and Vice President elect should die before March 4?

"(k) If more than three persons voted for as President should receive the highest number and an equal number of votes in the Electoral College, and suppose there were six candidates, three of whom had an equal number, who is to be preferred?

"(l) If there should be more than two of the candidates for the vice presidency in a similar category, for how many then, and for whom, would the Senate vote?

"(m) If a candidate for President should die after the election and before January 12 and before the electors met, how should they vote?

"(n) If the President should die after the Electoral College has met and before Congress counted the vote, how could the vote be counted? Or could it be postponed?

sentatives, the votes shall be taken by roll call of the Members, " and a majority of all the Representatives shall be necessary to a choice." In this manner the Members of the House vote as individual units and not as States. The proposal further provides that in the Senate a majority of the number of Senators shall be necessary to a choice for Vice President.[39]

17. The question of ex-Presidents.

The question has often been discussed as to " What shall we do with our ex-Presidents? " Having filled the highest office in the land it is a difficult matter for an ex-President to consider the acceptance of any inferior one thereafter, although the service of John Quincy Adams in the House of Representatives has clearly demonstrated the great use to which an ex-President can put the experience gathered in the White House. The only other

---

"(o) Should the Congress, particularly when repudiated by the people, continue to legislate? Or should a new Congress be convened of the people? And

" Whereas various constitutional amendments are pending in the Senate and House of Representatives providing in part a remedy for these situations: Therefore be it

" *Resolved,* That there shall be created a constitutional amendment commission, which shall consist of nine members, three of whom shall be appointed by the Speaker of the House of Representatives, three of whom shall be appointed by the President pro tempore of the Senate, and three of whom shall be appointed by the President of the United States.

" Sec. 2. The committee is authorized and directed to study these and other pertinent questions and to prepare the form and substance of necessary constitutional amendment or amendments, and to make final report and recommendation to Congress not later than January 1, 1926."

[39]App., No. 1362.

case of an ex-President being elected to Congress was that of Andrew Johnson who was elected to the Senate in 1875, but who died before taking the oath of office.

In an effort to settle this question, and definitely fix an ex-President's status, various proposed amendments to the Constitution have included provisions regarding this matter. Two amendments introduced in 1882 and 1884 included a provision for pensioning ex-Presidents.[40] The latter of these amendments may have been prompted by the pathetic condition of Grant's fortune in 1884, when the firm with which he was associated went bankrupt and he was left practically penniless.[41]

The passage by Congress of an act in 1885 creating ex-President Grant a general on the retired list has probably suggested to some legislators the feasibility of a constitutional amendment providing that ex-Presidents shall be borne on the retired list as if retiring from the Army or Navy. Being constitutionally commander in chief of the Army and Navy this would not necessarily be an anomaly in American institutions. Two such amendments were submitted by Mr. Hobson, of Alabama, in 1913.[42]

Four other proposals taking care of ex-Presidents stipulate that they shall become Senators at large with all the duties, privileges, and rights of a Senator.[43] One serious objection to this plan is that it would give the ex-President's home State a representation of three Senators, thus putting the other States to a disadvantage. A plan which would take care of this inequality in votes was embodied in the amendment proposed by Mr. De Armond, of Mis-

[40]Ames, p. 129.

[41] Coolidge, Louis. Life of President Grant, pp. 558–559.

[42]App., Nos. 665, 681.

[43]App., Nos. 777, 792, 827, 909.

souri, where the ex-President would become a Senator for life but with no vote.[44] It is doubted, however, whether a voteless Senator could demand the attention which would ordinarily be due an ex-President, and this would offer serious objections to ex-Presidents availing themselves of the privilege.

With but four exceptions, all of our Presidents have been over 50 years of age at the time of their inauguration.[45] Thus most Presidents leaving the White House are of an advanced age, and, with the weakened physical resistance usually brought about by the strenuous executive duties, it is generally not practicable for an ex-President actively to reenter civil life for remunerative employment. Considering also that the salary paid our Presidents is much less than that paid most rulers of nations, it can pretty well be assumed that the people would look with favor upon an amendment such as that presented by Mr. Buchanan, of Illinois, providing that all ex-Presidents shall be allowed the franking privilege and receive a pension equal to not less than one-third of the President's salary. Under this plan an ex-President could, if he desired, retire from active participation in civil and political life and thus be able to give unbiased opinions upon current problems based upon knowledge acquired while acting as President.[46]

Two of these resolutions make provision for the ex-Vice Presidents, giving them seats in the House of Representatives with all the privileges and rights of regularly elected members.[47]

---

[44] App., No. 128.

[45] Polk, 49; Garfield, 49; Cleveland, 47; Roosevelt, 42.

[46] App., No. 766.

[47] App., Nos. 827, 909.

18. The veto power.

There is no doubt that the framers of the Constitution believed that the veto power provided therein would be used but rarely. No English monarch had disapproved a bill of Parliament since 1708, and it was assumed that the President with his limited authority would not greatly use the privilege which the English king did not dare to use at all.[48] Realizing the tremendous power the President could exercise through the use of the veto, and fearing perhaps that sometimes it might be used to the country's disadvantage, an amendment was introduced in 1818 to deprive the President of the power of approving or disapproving bills. Such an amendment has been introduced on two other occasions, but there is very little chance, if any, of its ever being considered by the committee to which referred.[49]

Controversies between the President and Congress over vetoed legislation have led to the submission from time to time of resolutions designed to permit the repassage of an unapproved bill by a majority vote of both Houses, instead of the two-thirds vote now required. The difficulties experienced by Congress in dealing with Presidents Jackson and Tyler over desired legislation led to the submission between 1833 and 1842 of 10 amendments providing that a majority vote be sufficient to override a President's objection to a bill passed by Congress.[50] From 1842 to 1889 this proposal was offered six more times, but not actively pushed.[51]

[48] Mason, E. C. The Veto Power, pp. 1–23.
[49] Ames, p. 130. App., No. 608.
[50] Ames, p. 130.
[51] Ames, p. 132.

In 1896, however, an energetic attempt was made to have Congress favorably consider and pass such a resolution. This agitation was precipitated by President Cleveland's use of the veto power to an extent hitherto unknown.[52] It was asserted by many Members of Congress at this time that President Cleveland was stepping beyond his constitutional power, and that section 7 of Article I of the Constitution providing for the veto was intended merely as a means of protecting the executive office from encroachments by the legislature, and to prevent the passage of what appeared to him to be unconstitutional legislation.[53]

In the discussion of Cleveland's veto message on the rivers and harbors bill (H. R. 7977) of the Fifty-fourth Congress, Mr. Pettigrew, of South Dakota, denying that the President had the right to disapprove all bills sent to him, pointed out that with a faction of one-third of each House in back of him the President could effectively thwart legislation and thus establish a government by minority rule.[54] Mr. Stewart, of New Jersey, advanced the rather extreme view that everything else being equal Congress should always vote to pass a bill over the President's veto on the broad ground that the veto was an extraordinary and dangerous power and that all Members of Congress should join to sustain the bill passed by the constitutional majority.[55] Mr. Hill, of New York, indicated that the heart of the trouble lay in the fact that

[52] From 1885 to May 1, 1896, he vetoed 551 bills. Of these 542 were pension bills. From 1789 to 1885 the veto had been used but 109 times. Mr. Pettigrew's speech, Cong. Rec., June 3, 1896, p. 7977.

[53] See discussion in House. Cong. Rec., June 3, 1896.

[54] Cong. Rec., June 3, 1896, p. 6035.

[55] Cong. Rec., June 3, 1896, p. 6036.

the President was compelled to veto a whole bill when perhaps but a very few of its provisions were objectionable. To obviate this difficulty he recommended the passage of an amendment (S. Res. No. 156) permitting the President to disapprove all such items as he objected to, without interfering with the approval of the rest of the bill.[56]

Mr. Butler, of North Carolina, opposing the President, followed the introduction of Mr. Hill's resolution with one of his own providing for the overriding of a President's veto by a majority vote of Congress.[57] This proposition merely means that if, after listening to the President's objection to a bill already passed by both Houses, Congress is still in favor of it, the bill shall again be passed by a majority vote and become a law without the President's signature. Neither one of these resolutions ever came to a vote. The " majority overrule " amendment has been introduced three other times.[58]

With the exception of the attempts made in President Cleveland's administration to curtail the veto powers of the President, the tendency has been during the past half century to increase rather than decrease the President's prerogative in this respect.

In 1873 President Grant recommended to Congress the passage of an amendment authorizing " the Executive to approve of so much of any measure passing the two Houses as his judgment may dictate, without approving the whole, the disapproved portions or portion to be subject to the same rules as now." [59] Seventy amendments

[56]App., No. 198.

[57]App., No. 196.

[58]App., Nos. 148, 184, 655.

[59]Ames, pp. 132–133.

have been submitted since in the endeavor to add this proposition to the Constitution.[60]

In a speech on an amendment of this nature introduced by himself October 22, 1919, Mr. Hastings, of Oklahoma, stated that he had communicated with the governors of all the States regarding the gubernatorial veto power and that in not one instance did a governor give an unfavorable report on the separate-item veto. Eighteen of the States already had the provision in effect and four of these further allow the governor to reduce items in appropriation bills.[62]

Opponents of this plan contend that it would tend to mix the powers of the executive and legislative departments in a way that was never intended by the framers of the Constitution. Proponents of the plan reply that this argument is untenable for the reason that it is impossible to keep these two departments isolated from each other.[63] They point out further that the prerogatives given in the original Constitution to the President to recommend and approve or disapprove legislation indicates that the two departments must perforce work together.

[60]Ames, p. 133. App., Nos. 12, 25, 81, 146, 150, 171, 198, 199, 219, 229, 363, 371, 573, 682, 712, 726, 758, 767, 785, 807, 832, 848, 860, 867, 868, 872, 880, 915, 946, 983, 991, 1005, 1013, 1077, 1078, 1217, 1219, 1265, 1329.

[62] Cong. Rec., Apr. 22, 1920, pp. 6001–6006.

[63] While it is true that in one sense the governor when engaged in considering bills is acting in a legislative capacity and is for that purpose a part of the legislative department of the State (People *v.* Bowen, 21 N. Y. 521); he is exercising only a qualified and destructive legislative function, and not a creative legislative power." (Fergs *v.* Russel, 270 Ill. 304.)

19. Power of removal.

Owing to the differences which occasionally arose between the President and the Senate over the power of removal from Federal offices, from 1789 to 1889 15 amendments were introduced regulating and in general restricting the power of the President in this respect. None of these became effective and the only actual restriction put upon the President's power over Federal offices was the tenure of office act of 1867, which was wholly repealed in 1877.[64]

With the definite abandonment of the old-time "spoils system" there has been but little occasion to consider this subject, and although the Senate participates in the appointment of public officers it is now well settled that the power of removal is vested in the President alone.[65] Accordingly only two amendments touching this subject have been introduced during the last 40 years. These were presented, respectively, in 1905 and 1906 and declare that Congress shall have the power to remove all civil officers, other than the President and Vice President, by a concurrent vote of two-thirds of each House on account of immorality, imbecility, maladministration, misfeasance, or malfeasance in office.[66] An amendment introduced in December, 1926, by Mr. King, of Utah, provided that Congress shall have power to provide for the removal of officers of the United States except judges of the courts and heads of departments.[67]

[64] Ames, pp. 137–138.

[65] Hill, John P. The Federal Executive, p. 52.

[66] App., Nos. 412, 442.

[67] App., No. 1300.

20. Election of Executive officials.

The Constitution provides that with the consent of the Senate the President shall appoint all officers of the United States not otherwise provided for, but " Congress may by law vest the appointment of such inferior officers as they think proper, in the President alone, in the courts of law, or in the heads of departments. (Art. II, sec. 2, cl. 2.) Various resolutions have been introduced in the attempt to add to this the clause, " or the Congress may provide for the election by the people of such inferior officers in such manner as may be prescribed by law." [68]

From 1789 to 1888, 29 propositions were presented to amend the Constitution providing for the election of postmasters, revenue collectors, marshals, and other United States officers, except judges, whose duties required them to live in the State.[69] From 1889 to 1928, 12 amendments have been introduced with the same object in view.[70] Two of these stipulated that all officers inferior to judges of the Supreme Court should be elective.[71] One required all public officers except Cabinet members, ambassadors, ministers, and consuls to be elected, while another amendment of a radical nature (discussed in sec. 74) contemplated the election of every official in the United States Government.[72]

21. Abolition of life tenure.

Two of the amendments mentioned in the preceding section, in addition to the election of United States officers inferior to Supreme Court justices, provide for the

[68] App., No. 13.
[69] Ames, p. 142.
[70] App., Nos. 13, 44, 57, 114, 432, 450, 480, 483, 644, 770, 839, 912.
[71] App., Nos. 839, 912.
[72] App., No. 114.

abolishment of life tenure.[73] This, of course, applies chiefly to the judicial officers, for under the Constitution they are the only officials with no limited term of office. The amendments are so comprehensively worded, however, as to include any office that might furnish a life tenure for any occupant. House Joint Resolution No. 309,[74] introduced in the Sixty-third Congress, and House Joint Resolution No. 50,[75] introduced in the Sixty-fifth Congress by Mr. Moon, of Texas, were particularly designed to prevent life tenure by prohibiting any person from holding any office under the United States or any State government for a period longer than 15 years. An amendment presented in the Sixty-fourth Congress stipulated a limit of 10 years.[76]

Some political writers state that it is hardly to be expected that an amendment of this nature will be adopted. While the establishment of any system which might lead to autocratic control of any part of the Government is to be properly condemned, yet it can not be assumed, they say, that mere continuity in office will bring about autocracy, especially when that continuity is dependent upon the votes of others. The most efficient men in Congress are those that have had long service there, recognized by the practice of basing qualification for committee chairmanships mostly on seniority in office.[77] The appointive offices under the President, except those of the judiciary, are usually for a limited term coextensive with the Presi-

[73] App., Nos. 839, 912.

[74] App., No. 761.

[75] App., No. 912.

[76] App., No. 839.

[77] Munro, W. B. Government of United States, p. 154.

dent's, and thus hold out no tendencies toward usurpation of power. The matter of terms for judges is considered under section 25.

22. Pertaining to the Presidency.

From that clause in the Constitution which says the President shall recommend to Congress the consideration of such measures "as he shall judge necessary and expedient" (Art. II, sec. 3) has grown the political theory that he is responsible for the passage of needed public legislation. The President's executive duties in connection with legislation are not now confined to a mere recommendation that Congress *consider* the passage or rejection of certain contemplated laws. With the gradual development in strength of the presidential office and the expansion of his powers, the Executive now actively presses the *passage* of certain measures he deems necessary to the country's welfare.[78] This increase of the President's legislative prerogatives does not seem to have aroused much congressional opposition, but on the contrary there seems to be an appreciation of the need of a leader to shape the legislative policy of the country.[79] This realization was expressed in a rather extreme form in a resolution introduced by Senator Bristow, of Kansas, in 1912, providing that the Constitution should be amended to declare that in the event "Congress fails to enact any measure which the President has recommended in the proper form within six months from the date of such recommendation, the President at the next regular congressional election following the expiration of such period may submit the measure to the electors at such

[78] Hill. The Federal Executive, pp. 215–237.

[79] Wilson, Woodrow. Constitutional Government, pp. 54–76.

election, and if a majority of the congressional districts, and also if the majority of the State approve the measure, it shall become a law." [80]

The unfortunate extended illness of President Wilson during his second term led to the discussion once more of the question which had been agitated during President Garfield's period of illness, namely, Who is to determine whether the disability mentioned in Article II, section 1, clause 5, actually exists or not? [81] In an effort to avoid any future embarrassment on this point an amendment to the Constitution was proposed by Mr. Fess, of Ohio, declaring that the Supreme Court should be the tribunal to determine the question, and that the Supreme Court would convene for this purpose when authorized by a concurrent resolution of Congress. Further, that the Vice President was to be authorized to call Congress into special session with this object in view upon recommendation of the Cabinet.[82] He reintroduced this same resolution in 1921.[83]

The action of President Wilson in going to France led to the submission of an amendment declaring that in the event of the President's absence from the United States, or his death, resignation, or inability to serve, the Members and Members elect to the Senate and House of Representatives were authorized, upon a majority vote of both Houses or a three-fifths vote of either House, to convene in extraordinary session. Mr. Browne, of Wisconsin, introduced a similar resolution in 1923.[84]

---

[80] App., No. 658.

[81] Dougherty, Electoral System of the United States, p. 276.

[82] App., No. 1014

[83] App., No. 1038.

[84] App., No. 1196.

None of these resolutions was reported by the committee to which referred.

23. Succession to the Presidency.

The Constitution provides that in the event of the Presidency becoming vacated, the Vice President shall assume the office (Art. II, sec. 5), but this refers to a removal after the oath of office has been administered The presidential succession act of 1886 indicating the order in which members of the Cabinet accede to the Presidency in the event of the death of the President and Vice President also necessarily applies only after the administration has been formed and the President sworn in.[85] No provision is therefore made for the contingency of both the President and Vice President dying or becoming disabled before inauguration.[86]

That this is a real danger and should be met by a constitutional amendment is forcibly illustrated by the historical fact that Blaine died on January 29 after the presidential election of 1892. If he had been the successful candidate the casus omissus in the Constitution would have been evident.

> Had Lincoln on the way to the Capital for his inauguration met the fate which awaited him at Baltimore, no legal President could have ever after existed. The fact that four of our Presidents have died within a few weeks after their inauguration shows that the position is altogether a dangerous one.[87]

[85] Hamlin, C. S. Presidential Succession Act, Harvard Law Review, XVIII, p. 182.

[86] Dougherty, J. H. The Electoral System of the United States, p. 267.

[87] Statement by Albert W. Paine appended to H. Res. No. 144 introduced Mar. 19, 1896.

There is also the possibility that in a contested presidential election the House of Representatives and Senate may be so divided when there are three or more political parties in the field that neither a President nor Vice President could be elected; in which event, with the exception of the courts, the Federal Government could not function as there would be no executive to call a special session of Congress or to sign bills it might pass in the regular session.[88]

To supply this omission an amendment to the Constitution was proposed in 1896 by Mr. Boutelle, of Maine, which declared that in the event of the death of both the President and Vice President elect before inauguration, Congress shall determine who shall act as President for the ensuing term.[89] No action was taken on this proposal.

On January 18, 1898, a similar resolution was submitted by Senator Frye, of Maine, and it was referred to the Senate Committee on the Judiciary.[90] Senator Hoar, from that committee, reporting on the resolution, declared that it was not sufficiently comprehensive, as it did not cover the cases where by reason of a failure in the election machinery neither President nor Vice President have been elected. Such a failure nearly happened in the Burr-Jefferson election,[91] and despite Amendment XII to the Constitution, with three or more political parties contesting the election, it may happen again.[92] The com-

[88] Dougherty, p. 274.

[89] App., No. 189.

[90] App., No. 241.

[91] McClure, A. K. Our Presidents, and How We Make Them, pp. 12–20.

[92] Cong. Rec., Mar. 14, 1898, p. 2767.

mittee therefore substituted for Senator Frye's resolution the following:

> The provisions of Article II, clause 5, of the Constitution will remain in force and whenever there is no person entitled to discharge the duties of the office of President the same shall devolve upon the Vice President. The Congress may by law provide for the case where there is no person entitled to hold the office of President or Vice President, declaring what officer shall then act as President, and such officer shall act accordingly until the disability shall be removed or a President shall be elected.

On May 4, 1898, this resolution was further amended so that the first part read: "In all cases not provided for by Article II, clause 5, of the Constitution, where there is no, etc.," and in this form it passed the Senate by a unanimous vote.[93]

Twenty-four other resolutions embodying practically the same principle in varying forms have since been presented in Congress.[94]

In speaking of the need of an amendment of this nature Senator Bacon, of Georgia, said:

> It is simply to provide against the possibility of a vacancy in the office of President without any provision of law for filling it. I never heard any Senator object to it in any way.[95]

On May 16, 1910, this proposition was voted down in the House, but as it was connected up with many other provisions which the House particularly objected to, it can not be assumed that the vote was a rejection of this individual feature of the resolution.[96]

---

[93] Cong. Rec., May 4, 1898, p. 4574.

[94] App., Nos. 339, 429, 445, 513, 552, 555, 603, 612, 613, 625, 641, 1284, 1288, 1289, 1272, 1278, 1309, 1318, 1323, 1328, 1333, 1340, 1351.

[95] Cong. Rec., Feb. 1, 1909, p. 1680.

[96] Cong. Rec., May 6, 1910, p. 6368. App., No. 555.

On December 5, 1927, Mr. Lea introduced a resolution which provided inter alia that where Congress has given to the President or President elect the power to determine who shall act as president because of the death or disability of the President, Vice President, President elect, and Vice President elect, such person's designation shall be confirmed by the Senate before he may take office to act in that capacity until a President shall have been elected.[97]

Three resolutions presented in 1923 declared that if the House of Representatives has not chosen a President by Inauguration Day, the Vice President shall act as President.[98] Two of these go further and state that if the Vice President has not been elected by the Senate, Congress shall then declare who shall act as President until the House of Representatives chooses a President or the Senate a Vice President.[99]

An amendment passed in the Senate on March 18, 1924, (S. J. Res. No. 22) provided that if the House of Representatives did not choose a President by March 4, then the Vice President would become President for the term, and that if a Vice President was not chosen before the time fixed for the beginning of his term, Congress should choose the officer to act as President until a President or Vice President be elected by the House of Representatives or Senate, respectively.

Two resolutions designed to bring about a thorough study of the questions involved in this section were introduced in 1924.[1]

---

[97]App., No. 1309.

[98]App., Nos. 1171, 1208, 1215.

[99]App., Nos. 1171, 1208.

[1] See sec. 16.

24. Vice Presidents.

The death of six of our Presidents while in office and the death of six Vice Presidents indicate that at many times in our history the country has been without a Vice President.[2] That a double death did not occur in any one administration has been the good fortune of the Nation, but in an attempt to provide for such a contingency many resolutions have been introduced in Congress prescribing various methods for filling vacancies in the presidential and vice presidential chairs. In 1881 a resolution was presented providing for the creation of a first, second, and third Vice President. From 1881 to 1889, five more were introduced providing for a second Vice President only.[3] This officer was to be elected at the same time with the President and the Vice President.

Since 1889 four amendments have been submitted declaring that the President pro tempore of the Senate should accede to the Vice Presidency when that office becomes vacant.[4]

On January 4, 1909, Mr. Burke, of Pennsylvania, introduced a resolution providing that Congress shall determine who is to be President in the event of the death of the Vice President, and, if deemed necessary, to call a special election for the purpose of choosing a President.[5] Another amendment of a similar nature was presented September 11, 1914, and declared that if both the Presi-

[2] Harrison, 1841; Taylor, 1850; Lincoln, 1865; Garfield, 1881; McKinley, 1901; Harding, 1923. Vice Presidents: Gerry, 1814; King, 1853; Wilson, 1875; Hendricks, 1885; Hobart, 1899; Sherman, 1912.

[3] Ames, p. 72. App., No. 18.

[4] App., Nos. 248, 258, 362, 517.

[5] App., No. 515.

dent and Vice President became disabled Congress was empowered to hold a special election to choose a Chief Magistrate unless the deaths occurred within one year of the next regular election.[6]

It has frequently been asserted that the Vice President should occupy a more determinative position in the Government's administration than merely presiding officer of the Senate where he is allowed neither the privilege of debate nor vote.[7] In an amendment covering this subject, introduced in 1916 by Mr. Hayes of California, provision was made that the Vice President should be ex officio a member of the Cabinet without portfolio.[8]

---

[6]App., No. 766.

[7] Roosevelt, Theodore. American Ideals, pp. 189–194. Discussing this subject President Roosevelt said: " The Vice President should, so far as possible, represent the same views and principles which have secured the nomination and election of the President, and he should be a man standing well in the councils of the party, trusted by his fellow party leaders, and able in the event of any accident to his chief to take up the work of the latter where it was left. One sure way to secure this desired result would undoubtedly be to increase the power of the Vice President. He should always be a man who would be consulted by the President on every great party question. It would be well if he were given a seat in the Cabinet. It might be well if, in addition to his vote in the Senate in the event of a tie, he should be given a vote on ordinary occasions and perchance on occasions a voice in the debates."

[8]App., No 827.

CHAPTER III

PROPOSED AMENDMENTS AFFECTING THE FORM OF THE JUDICIARY DEPARTMENT

25. Term of judges.

During the first 100 years of American constitutional history the judiciary department has been subjected to fewer attacks by proposed constitutional amendments than either of the other two departments. The only proposition which received any considerable attention was that declaring for the limiting of judges' terms to a certain number of years. The fact that the life tenure of judges was accepted unanimously by the Convention of 1787 to a certain extent deterred the thought that there was anything inherently dangerous to republican institutions in a life judiciary.[1] Nevertheless, in some form or other a score of attempts have been made during the first century to add to the Constitution an amendment providing for a limited term of office for all Federal judges.[2]

During the last 39 years this idea has progressed considerably and no less than 39 attempts have been made to incorporate it in some fashion or other into the organic law. The main argument advanced by supporters of this innovation is that the ideal entertained by the framers of the Constitution that a life tenure would give Federal

[1] Watson, David K. The Constitution of the United States, p. 1069.

[2] Ames, pp. 151–152.

judges independence and impartiality has not been realized. It is further contended that with the retiring age placed at the advanced age of 70 years,[3] it frequently happens a judge is kept in office long after he has become, by reason of physical infirmities, incapable of giving the considerate attention to the work which a judgeship demands. Sometimes special acts of Congress have been necessary to retire judges physically unfit for a continuation of their work.[4]

In introducing his amendment in 1912 proposing to limit judges' terms to 10 years, Senator Crawford, of South Dakota, said:

> The irritation and the uneasiness of the people and their hostility to the courts are directed largely against these inferior Federal courts and the amendment I propose would be accepted by three-fourths of the States because of a prevailing opinion that some of these Federal judges are too indifferent to the rights of the people and not sufficiently responsive to the present-day needs and present-day conditions when passing upon issues between the people and public interests. The fact that at the expiration of a fixed term his conduct as a judge would come under review by the President and the Senate both of them, when determining whether or not he should be reappointed, acting under the scrutinizing and watchful eye of the people, would not threaten his independence, but would operate as a wholesome restraint upon the judge, while the expiration of his term would furnish the opportunity to dispense with the services of an unworthy or incompetent man. (Cong. Rec., May 12, 1912, p. 6999.)

Those opposed to the limited term deny that there is political activity among the United States judges, and that the little political prejudice and zeal a lawyer takes with him upon the bench is soon lost sight of and for-

---

[3]Ames, p. 151, citing R. S. 1878, sec. 714.

[4] H. Rept. No. 446, 53d Cong., 2d sess.

gotten by himself as well as the public in the impartial discharge of his high office; but that if there is, "what justifies the presumption that a change of tenure of office to 10 years will do away with it?"[6]

To the argument that the judges are too far removed from responsibility to any authority it is answered that if their reappointment is made to depend upon the will of some one else, "they would not exercise their own untrammeled judgment, but they would execute the will of the person to whom they are responsible.[7]

Most of the amendments declaring for the popular election of Federal judges include provisions for a limited term of office.[8] Twelve amendments have been presented limiting the term of office but retaining the present method of appointment.[9] The length of term prescribed in these amendments ranges from 6 to 12 years (only one prescribes 4 years),[10] with the 10-year period predominating. Eight provide that Congress shall designate the term of office.[11]

26. Removal of judges.

In 1805 John Randolph, of Virginia, introduced in Congress an amendment declaring United States judges to be subject to removal from office by the President on the joint address of both Houses of Congress. This amendment was prompted by the House's failure in that

---

[6] H. Rept. No. 466, 53d Cong., 2d sess., Mr. Stone.

[7] Ibid.

[8] App., Nos. 239, 266, 352, 396, 450, 452, 460, 466, 476, 480, 644, 628, 634, 640, 644, 646, 683, 688, 740, 761, 768, 771, 786, 839, 1016.

[9] App., Nos. 139, 616, 637, 675, 799, 753, 773, 852, 921, 945, 947, 995.

[10] App., No. 771.

[11] App., Nos. 466, 476, 235, 352, 396, 947, 995, 1081.

year to secure a conviction against Judge Chase.[12] Fifteen other amendments referring to the removal of Federal judges have been submitted from 1805 to 1889.[13]

As at present established, judges of the Federal judiciary hold office during good behavior, and as the machinery of impeachment is a hard one to move, this makes the judge's term generally a life tenure. It has, therefore, been maintained by many legislators that there should be some way not so difficult as the impeachment process for the removal of objectionable judges.[14] Some of the amendments providing for the popular election of judges include the recall feature.[15]

On the subject of the removal of judges the amendment introduced most numerously in recent times is that stipulating for the removal of a judge by a two-thirds concurring vote of both Houses of Congress. This amendment has been presented four times.[16]

One resolution introduced in 1912 by Senator Ashurst, of Arizona, provided that a judge of an inferior court could be recalled by the qualified electors of the district in which such judge may have committed treason, bribery, or other high crimes or misdemeanors,[17] while another amendment presented in 1913 by Senator Pomerene, of Ohio, was designed to protect the Supreme Court from the provisions of any legislation that changed the removal of justices from that bench by any means except the present method of impeachment.[18]

---

[12] Bruce, Wm. C. Life of John Randolph, pp. 201–206.

[13] Ames, pp. 148–149.

[14] Baldwin, Simeon E. The American Judiciary, pp. 340–343.

[15] App., Nos. 628, 688.

[16] App., Nos. 648, 662, 722, 1142.

[17] App., No. 649.

[18] App., No. 667.

27. Election of judges.

In 1867 Mr. Cobb, of Wisconsin, introduced the first amendment designed to give Congress the power to designate whether judges of the inferior courts of the United States and Territories should be appointed or elected.[19] Since then such an amendment has been submitted ten times.[20]

Numerous other resolutions have been introduced specifically stating that all judges of the inferior courts shall be elected by the people—that is, by the electors in the circuits and districts for which the judge shall be chosen.[21] Thirteen of these designated that the judges of the Supreme Court should also be elected by the people,[22] the associate justices to be chosen by the electors of the circuits to which they have been assigned, and the Chief Justice to be elected by all the electors qualified to vote for Representatives in Congress. Of this group, two provided that the Chief Justice be chosen by the associate justices from their number.[23]

Despite these many attempts to provide for the popular election of Federal judges it is very improbable that they will be so chosen. Only once was a report rendered by the committee to which these resolutions were referred, and that report was an unfavorable one.[24]

[19]Ames, p. 146.

[20]App., Nos. 235, 266, 352, 396, 634, 646, 740, 786, 466, 483.

[21]App., Nos. 266, 289, 404, 450, 452, 460, 476, 545, 628, 640, 644, 683, 688, 761, 768, 771, 839, 912, 1016, 1241, 1295.

[22]App., Nos. 114, 289, 404, 450, 452, 460, 480, 483, 545, 628, 644, 688, 1016.

[23]App., Nos. 483, 450.

[24]App., No. 289.

28. Judges to be ineligible to other offices.

With the heavy pressure of work all Federal judges are subjected to, there is now very little possibility of their accepting any other office under the United States. During the early days of the Federal judiciary when the business of the courts was not so pressing, it was not incompatible with the office of a judgeship for the occupant thereof to be appointed to some special mission of a non-judiciary nature. In 1794 Chief Justice Jay was appointed as a special envoy to England, and in 1799 Chief Justice Ellsworth was chosen as one of the three commissioners to France. This awakened the fear that a judge might become too much aligned with political interests for the proper discharge of his unpartisan judicial duties.[25] An amendment was accordingly introduced "restricting judges from holding any other office or appointment whatever."[26] This proposition has been renewed but four times since, the last one being submitted by Mr. Mercer, of Nebraska, in 1893, providing that a Federal judge is "disqualified to stand as candidate for and to hold and enjoy any other office of profit under the United States during his official incumbency."[27]

The acceptance by Justice Hughes of the Republican presidential nomination in 1916 was doubtless the reason that actuated the presentation on June 13 of that year of an amendment declaring that a judge should not be qualified to accept any elective office under the United

[25] See Warren, Chas. History of United States Supreme Court.
[26] Ames, pp. 147–148.
[27] App., No. 133.

States during his incumbency or within two years after its expiration.[28]

29. Composition of courts.

Article III, section 2, of the Constitution provides that " The judicial power of the United States shall be vested in one Supreme Court, and in such inferior courts as the Congress may from to time ordain and establish." As Congress has power under this provision to create and abolish inferior courts and declare the number of judges that shall constitute the Supreme Court, only two amendments have so far been introduced on this subject. One in 1880 provided for the addition to the third article: " The Supreme Court of the United States shall consist of a Chief Justice of the United States and —— associate judges, and —— of which shall constitute a quorum," [29] and another in 1898 declared that the Supreme Court shall consist of not less than 9 Supreme Court judges and not more than 13.[30]

30. Jurisdiction of the courts.

Owing to the monopolization of the export trade of the Colonies by the mother country England, and the fact that there was no universal law to protect the credit of citizens doing business in a State other than their own, commercial intercourse between the people of the various Colonies was not on a very large scale. As a means of stimulating this intercourse and thus making the entire country more cooperative and self-supporting, the provi-

---

[28] Article in Literary Digest, " For and Against Justice Hughes," vol. 52 [2]; 1619–20, June, 1916. App., No. 847.

[29] Ames, p. 145.

[30] App., No. 239.

sion was included in section 2 of Article III of the Constitution that the jurisdiction of the Federal courts should extend to controversies between citizens of different States.[31] Another reason for this jurisdiction was that in controversies involving citizens of different States a State court might appear to be biased in favor of its own citizens, and thus that willingness to be bound by an unbiased tribunal might be lacking. Further it was considered that this uniform adjustment of controversies between citizens of different States, supplemented by the "Full faith and credit" clause of Article IV, would tend to foster that good commercial relationship upon which progress and prosperity depend.[32]

Some of the States have, however, felt aggrieved at the extensive jurisdiction given the Federal judiciary, and a feeling of jealousy early manifested itself in proposed amendments to the Constitution curtailing the jurisdiction of Federal courts.

The clause which gave the Federal courts the most business was that one covering controversies between citizens of different States. As early as the First Congress a proposal was advanced to limit Federal jurisdiction in such causes only to cases where the subject matter in dispute was of the value of $1,500.[33] Two other amendments limiting Federal jurisdiction were introduced in the First Congress, but they were given but little attention.[34]

The decision in the famous case of Chisholm *v.* Georgia[35] brought about the ratification of the eleventh

---

[31] Bacon, Charles W. American Plan of Government, p. 385.

[32] Bryce, American Commonwealth, p. 231.

[33] Ames, p. 154.

[34] Ames, pp. 154–155.

[35] 2 Dall. 419.

amendment to the Constitution, but this was not considered by some as a sufficient limitation to the Federal jurisdiction.[36] Accordingly, two amendments were introduced in 1805 and 1807 declaring that:

> The judicial power of the United States shall not be construed to extend to controversies between a State and the citizens of another State; between citizens of different States; between citizens of the same State claiming land under grants of different States; and between a State and the citizens thereof and foreign States, citizens or subjects.[37]

After this for almost 100 years, with but one exception,[38] there was no agitation for reducing the jurisdiction of the Federal courts. On the contrary, during this period two amendments were introduced calculated to increase the jurisdiction. The first one in 1872 provided that the Supreme Court should have original jurisdiction of all cases involving the constitutionality of a Federal law, and the second one in 1883 was intended to repeal the eleventh amendment.[39]

In 1898, in an amendment providing for the popular election of Federal judges, there was included a section denying to the Federal judiciary jurisdiction over controversies between citizens of different States.[40] Mr. Butler, of North Carolina, the originator of this resolution, reintroduced it in 1899.[41] This seemed to be the beginning of another effort to curtail Federal jurisdiction,

[36] Singewald, Karl. The Doctrine of Non-Suability of the States in the United States, Ch. II, pp. 15–26.

[37] Ames, p. 158.

[38] An amendment to restrict Federal jurisdiction was presented in 1882. Ames, p. 158.

[39] Ames, p. 159.

[40] App., No. 239.

[41] App., No. 289.

although commencing with 1904 the wording of the resolution was changed so that the restriction of jurisdiction applied to controversies between corporations instead of citizens.

With the establishment of the doctrine that the citizenship of the individuals composing a corporation is to be conclusively presumed to be that of the State by which the company was chartered the Federal courts have come into a very extensive jurisdiction, which in some cases the State courts would prefer to have themselves.[42]

In an effort to reduce some of this jurisdiction Mr. Russell, of Texas, introduced a resolution in 1904 declaring that the judicial power of the Federal courts "shall not be construed to extend to any suit between citizens of the different States unless such citizens are natural persons, nor where said suit or case shall be for the benefit of or shall in any wise affect any corporations whatever." [43] During the next four years he reintroduced a like resolution three times.[44]

Senator Overman, of North Carolina, presented a similar amendment in 1910, and then Mr. Raker, of California, from 1911 to 1917, offered for eight times the proposition that the "judicial power shall not be construed to extend to any suit in law or equity by reason of citizenship of any corporation." [45]

The only direct efforts made to increase the jurisdiction of the Federal courts occurred in 1901, when Senator Stewart, of Nevada, introduced a resolution providing that

[42] Willoughby, Constitutional Law, p. 413, citing Ohio & Mississippi R. R. Co. *v.* Wheeler, 1 Black, 286.

[43] App., No. 403.

[44] App., Nos. 453, 462, 546.

[45] App., Nos. 558, 598, 599, 690, 691, 787, 788, 885, 886.

the "judicial power of the United States shall extend to all controversies in law and equity relating to the use of water, except where the water and the use thereof are in the same State,"[46] and in 1916, when Mr. Taggart, of Kansas, attempted to bring about a uniform method of conducting trials and inflicting punishment for murder and manslaughter throughout the United States, by declaring that in all such cases the courts of the United States shall have exclusive jurisdiction.[47]

31. Power of the Supreme Court to declare laws unconstitutional.

The power of the Supreme Court to declare laws unconstitutional comes not from any such expressed grant in the Constitution, and it must be considered an implied power.[48] There is some historical contention as to whether the framers of the Constitution intended the Supreme Court to exercise such an authority.[49] Thus, although Chief Justice Marshall in Marbury *v.* Madison[50] stated in no uncertain terms that one of the duties of the Federal courts was to declare void all laws "repugnant to the Constitution," it does not seem that this decision settled everybody's mind on the subject.[51] In this respect we find the Supreme Court as late as 1895, in the Pollock *v.* Farmers' Loan & Trust Co.[52] decision, devoting more

[46] App., No 342.

[47] App., No. 822.

[48] Moore, B. F. The Supreme Court and Unconstitutional Legislation. Columbia University, 1913. Vol. LIV, No. 2, p. 36.

[49] Ibid., 34.

[50] 1 Cranch's Rep. 137.

[51] Moore. See Chapter 11, Attitude of Supreme Court toward declaring statutes unconstitutional, pp. 35–76.

[52] 157 U. S. Rep. 430.

than a page of the opinion to proving its right to declare laws unconstitutional.[53]

Accordingly the aggrieved parties in disputed issues where the Supreme Court has exercised this power have considered the feasibility of a tribunal higher than the Supreme Court. This has been especially true in cases where the Supreme Court has declared State laws unconstitutional and where, in disputes between the Federal Government and some State governments, the court has declared in favor of the former. Three amendments on this subject were proposed between 1789 and 1867. One provided for a commission to be appointed by the President,[54] one for an impartial tribunal to be made up of Federal and State officers,[55] and the third declared that the Senate should act as an appellate tribunal to review certain contested cases on which the Supreme Court had rendered decision.[56] It does not appear that any of these propositions received much favorable consideration by Congress.

During the last 15 years some agitation has arisen over the power exercised by the Supreme Court in declaring laws of Congress in conflict with the Constitution and thus void.[57] The large number of cases in which one or two less than the majority of justices have dissented from the majority decision declaring a law unconstitutional,[58] has

---

[53] Moore, p. 51.

[54] Ames, p. 159.

[55] Ibid., p. 160.

[56] Ibid., p. 161.

[57] Warren, Chas. History of Supreme Court. (See chapter 11.) Attacks upon Judicial Control, pp. 1–15.

[58] Moore, Supreme Court and Unconstitutional Legislation. (App. 1, pp. 129–130.)

led to the introduction of four amendments providing for a larger majority on such a decision before the Federal law in question may be declared ineffective. Senator Reed, of Missouri, in 1913 offered an amendment to the effect that no Federal law could be declared unconstitutional unless two-thirds of the court so agreed.[59] An amendment introduced by Mr. Hayden, of Arizona, in 1917, in 1919, and again in 1921, declared the Supreme Court incapable of declaring a law unconstitutional unless at least all but two of the judges concur in such decision.[60]

In 1912 an amendment was introduced with the unusual provision that if a law is declared unconstitutional by the Supreme Court it shall be submitted by the Secretary of State to the governors of the several States, accompanied by a proposed amendment to the Constitution making the law in question constitutional and valid. These two propositions are to be voted on by the legislatures of the States, and if three-fourths of the States declare the law constitutional it shall be so considered and the proposed amendment immediately become effective. If, however, the amendment is approved and the law rejected the amendment shall be valid as part of the Constitution from the date of its approval.[61] This amendment was reintroduced in 1914, but no action was taken on it.[62]

The initiative and referendum movement of recent years has led to the presentation of two amendments call-

[59]App., No. 675.

[60]App., Nos. 903, 977, 1041. The decisions in the Legal Tender cases show how the mere change of one or two justices may determine the constitutionality or unconstitutionality of a law. (Putney, Const. Law, pp. 241–246.)

[61]App., No. 653.

[62]App., No. 748.

ing for a popular determination of laws declared unconstitutional by the Supreme Court.[63] Both of these were submitted by Senator Bristow, of Kansas, and provide that Congress shall have power to submit such a disputed law to the electors at a regular congressional election, and that a majority of the electors voting thereon in a majority of the congressional districts and States approving same shall make it effective.

An amendment proposed in 1917 declared the Supreme Court should have no power to declare unconstitutional a law signed by the President, but where the court declared unconstitutional a law passed over the President's veto Congress had merely to repass it by a two-thirds vote to make it constitutional and effective.[64]

Another amendment introduced in 1923 provided that Congress shall have power to determine how many members of the Supreme Court shall join in declaring a law unconstitutional.[65]

An amendment proposed by Mr. Berger, of Wisconsin, in 1911 proposed that the House of Representatives should have final authority over all laws, and prohibit any court from declaring a law unconstitutional.[66]

[63]App., Nos. 668, 676.
[64]App., No. 869.
[65]App., No. 1142.
[66]App., No. 608.

Chapter IV

PROPOSED AMENDMENTS AFFECTING THE POWERS OF THE GOVERNMENT

32. Powers of Congress.

Always looked upon as a life guard whose services were to be freely given when civic and political rights were in danger, there has been a tendency in recent years toward empowering Congress with the duties and responsibilities of a coast patrol bound to guard and protect all jurisdiction where assumed rights—civic, social, and commercial—may go aground. This is apparent not only in the tremendous scope embraced in the thousands of bills introduced in each session of Congress but especially in the number and variety of resolutions proposing amendments to the Constitution to enlarge that scope. Innumerable subjects embracing fields of regulation and conflict between contending interests, which the respective States perhaps originally intended should always remain under their control, are now introduced in Congress for disposition. Labor, religion, education, temperance, marriage, divorce, monopolies, crime are only a few of the subjects which are urged upon Congress for control and regulation.

One resolution introduced in 1910, by Mr. Madden, of Illinois, is of such comprehensive scope that it is impossible to classify it elsewhere, so I give it alone:

"Section 1. Congress is hereby empowered to provide by law for the punishment of kidnaping, pandering, bigamy, polygamy, and conspiracy in restraint of trade, concurrent with the legislatures of the several States; also, to provide by law respecting the liability of employers for injuries to employees and for the adjustment, by arbitration or otherwise, of controversies and differences between capital and labor, and with the regulation or prevention of child labor, also concurrent with the several States."

Section 2 is in the nature of a bill of rights depriving the States of those powers denied the Federal Government in the first 10 amendments.

Section 3 gives Congress power to make laws " respecting the construction and regulation of water power, forests, minerals, and other natural resources, also respecting insurance paper, insurance, income, and inheritance taxes, marriage, divorce, and alimony."

Section 4 declares that the States shall retain the income and inheritance taxes collected therein, except in the event of war or great emergency, when Congress shall direct its use.[1]

In 1911, Mr. Buchanan, of Illinois, and in 1919 Mr. Watson, of Pennsylvania, introduced amendments of a paternalistic nature. The one gave Congress power to enact laws respecting compensation for personal injuries sustained by employees while working for private employers or in public work.[2] The other empowered Congress to regulate wages, hours of labor, and prices of commodities in the United States.[3]

Another amendment of a like nature was presented during the war by Mr. LaGuardia, of New York, and conferred upon Congress power to regulate the production, conservation, and distribution of foodstuffs and fuel. As Congress has this regulatory power during war time, it is assumed the amendment was intended to confer a permanent power.[4]

---

[1]App., No. 566.
[2]App., No. 604.
[3]App., No. 957.
[4]App., No. 922.

Two amendments were presented in 1908 concerning employers' liability. One was introduced by Mr. Ferris, of Oklahoma, and provided that Congress should have power to regulate the liability of common carriers, engaged in interstate or foreign commerce, to their servants or employees for injuries resulting from the negligence of fellow servants or employees. It also guaranteed the respective States the right to regulate intrastate railroad rates, as well as regulate and prohibit the products of convict labor coming into the State from other States.[5] The second one, presented by Senator Owen, of Oklahoma, merely gave Congress power to regulate employers' liability.[6]

In 1890 Senator Chandler, of New Hampshire, submitted an amendment designed to take the Federal power directly into the exclusive criminal jurisdiction of the States. It stipulated that when States fail to enact or effectually enforce laws against murder and other felonies Congress "may provide for punishing those crimes within such States."[7] On the same order was the resolution introduced by Mr. Emerson, of Ohio, in 1919, designed to give Congress power to enact laws to prevent lynching.[8]

An amendment of a unique nature and standing alone is that introduced by Senator McLean, of Connecticut, in 1911, and providing that Congress shall have power "to protect migratory birds and prohibit the killing thereof."[9]

In 1922 Mr. Volstead, of Minnesota, presented an amendment proposing to empower Congress to regulate

[5] App., No. 507.
[6] App., No. 508.
[7] App., No. 30.
[8] App., No. 970.
[9] App., No. 614.

the production of and commerce in the coal, oil, and gas from which interstate and foreign commerce are supplied.[10]

In 1922 and 1923 six amendments were proposed giving Congress the power to regulate the nomination and election of Senators and Representatives.[11]

The charges made during the Sixty-seventh Congress regarding the lavish expenditure of funds by candidates for senatorial and congressional offices was probably the cause for the introduction in that Congress and the following Congresses of the eight resolutions which provided that the Constitution should be amended to give Congress the power to prohibit corrupt practices and to regulate and limit all expenditures made or incurred by candidates for the office of Senator or Representative.[12]

In 1921 Mr. Herrick, of Oklahoma, introduced a resolution declaring that any election at which a candidate is nominated for or elected to a Federal office shall be deemed a Federal election and all Federal laws governing elections shall be extended to such election.[13]

In order that Congress may adjust the presidential and congressional terms to better fit into a plan to curtail the time which now exists between the date of election and the date Congress convenes, Mr. Lea, of California, included in the resolution presented by him on December 4, 1927, the provision that Congress shall have power to reduce the terms of the President, Vice President, Senators, and Representatives not more than two months.[14]

Some legislators feel that the Federal Government, in exercising supervisory and regulatory power over trans-

[10]App., No. 1121.

[11]App., Nos. 1112, 1141, 1162, 1168, 1170, 1203.

[12]App., Nos. 1095, 1106, 1158, 1205, 1354, 1355, 1357, 1358.

[13]App., No. 1083.

[14]App., No. 1309.

portation entirely within a State, even though definitely related to interstate or foreign commerce, is exceeding the powers intended to be given it by the Federal Constitution in the interstate clause. It is for this reason probably that Senator Mayfield, of Texas, on March 1, 1927, introduced his resolution providing that the power of Congress to regulate commerce shall not extend to the transportation of passengers or goods when such transportation begins and ends within the same State, and that no regulation prescribed by State authority for intrastate transportation shall be set aside by Congress because of its relation to, or effect upon, interstate or foreign commerce.[15]

33. Bearing of weapons.

The second amendment to the Constitution provides that " the right of the people to keep and bear arms shall not be infringed." As this is a limitation on the Federal Government, as, indeed, all of the first eight amendments are,[16] Congress is without the complete jurisdiction exercised by the States on this subject. In order to make up this deficiency, he considering that there is now no reason for the limitation, Mr. Park, of Georgia, twice introduced in 1913 a resolution to the effect that the second amendment should be added to, to permit Congress, within the Territories and the District of Columbia, to regulate and prohibit the carrying of concealed weapons, and to guarantee to the States the same privilege.[17]

34. Impeachment.

Under the Constitution the House of Representatives and the Senate, respectively, have the sole power of bring-

[15] App., No. 1308.

[16] Presser *v.* Illinois, 116 U. S. 252.

[17] App., Nos. 732, 737.

ing and trying impeachments. (Art. I, sec. 2, cl. 5; Art. I, sec. 3, cl. 6.) The execution of this duty has at times proved not only onerous but unsatisfactory.[18] Two attempts have thus been made to give Congress more latitude in impeachment proceedings. The first one of this group declared that Congress may provide by law for other methods of impeachment and trial for all civil officers of the United States, except the President, Vice President, and members of the Supreme Court.[19] The second amendment declared that the Senate may provide for the trial of all impeachments (except of the President, Vice President, and Chief Justice) by 12 Senators, the concurrence of 8 of whom shall be sufficient for conviction.[20] Under this latter amendment the Senate would not be seriously disturbed in the conduct of its regular business, as is true under the present procedure when the entire body must sit in hearing on a trial which frequently lasts for months.[21]

35. Land legislation.

The clearly observable trend of the American population from the farm to the city has awakened a fear in the minds of many that unless something is done to check this movement, in time a dangerous diminution in the food supply of the country will appear. Allied to this apprehension is the thought that with the rapidly growing centralization of wealth in a few persons, the family home, from which the Nation gathers its strength, will commence to disappear.

[18] Watson, David K. The Constitution of the United States, pp. 15–22.

[19] App., No. 667.

[20] App., No. 668.

[21] Beard, American Government, pp. 265–266.

In a speech on this subject in the Senate, June 12, 1917, Senator Sheppard, of Texas, pointed out that of the 20,000,000 families in the United States nearly 11,000,000 owned no homes at all, and that less than 6,000,000 owned homes free from incumbrance. Also, that while in 1870 more than 90 per cent of the people resided in the rural districts, in 1917 more than 50 per cent were crowded in the cities. Further, that of the arable area of the United States hardly one-half is occupied, and hardly half of the half occupied is under cultivation. In order to induce more people to live on farms and thus make the country more self-sustaining, he recommended that the United States inaugurate a constructive land policy which would have for its object the lending of Federal aid to those inclined toward farm cultivation, but who were without funds to carry on the work. All of the leading countries of the world and four of our States have already taken definite legislative steps toward enabling the people to acquire and maintain homes,[22] he pointed out.

The Federal farm loan act is a step in this direction, but some say it does not go far enough since many of those who would desire to avail themselves of its provisions do not have the security required by this law. To supply the deficiency Senator Sheppard recommended the passage of an amendment to the Constitution giving Congress power to purchase, improve, subdivide, and sell land anywhere in the United States, and also to make loans "for the purpose of encouraging and promoting farm homes in the United States." [23]

[22] Cong. Rec., June 12, 1917, p. 3513.
[23] App., No. 920.

This same amendment he had introduced a year before,[24] at which time, when the Senate was considering Senate bill No. 2986 to provide credits for the farmers, he asserted that "a vast and growing number of American farmers are reduced to such conditions that they have no land that they might offer as such security for loans of balances due on purchases, and hardly enough left after the landlord, the merchant, and the banker are paid from the proceeds of their crops to keep body and soul together until another crop is made." [25]

An amendment of a very unusual nature on this subject is one offered by Mr. Thayer, of Massachusetts, January 21, 1914. It provides generally that the United States shall take over from all persons holding over 12 acres of land that surplus and give to all other persons 8 contiguous acres each, adding that at every census, United States' or world's, the fertile land shall again be divided up so that each person will have an equal share.[26]

In March, 1925, Mr. Lankford, of Georgia, proposed two amendments of a paternalistic nature, one providing that all lands and improvements thereon owned by farmers and livestock growers are to be exempt from taxation up to the actual equity of the owner in the property in question; the other declaring that no tax or occupation charge shall be assessed against any farmer or livestock grower engaging in the sale of food products directly to the consumer.[27]

[24] App., No. 841, Apr. 28, 1916.

[25] Cong. Rec. Apr. 28, 1916, p. 6947.

[26] App., No. 401.

[27] App., Nos. 1255, 1256.

36. Marriage and divorce.

That the States have absolute jurisdiction over the subjects of marriage and divorce there can be no doubt. No direct mention thereof is made in the Constitution; and the only indirect reference, that which prohibits a State from the impairment of contractual obligations (Art. I, sec. 10), has been construed not to refer to the matrimonial relation.[28]

The difference in ideas in the various States as to what constitutes the qualifications for marriage and the sufficient causes for divorce have naturally brought about a confusion of standards in this respect throughout the United States. These differences, which originated through the variety of laws of the various countries from which our territory has been acquired, have been fixed and added to by custom and expediency until now the law as to void, voidable, and prohibited marriages is different in almost every State of the Union.[29]

In an effort to harmonize all these conflicting laws and ideas regarding marriage and divorce and thus bring about a homogeneous, definitely fixed marital status, a great number of proposals have been made to amend the Constitution in this regard. It was not until the second half of the nineteenth century, however, when the improved methods of transportation and the heavy increase in commercial intercourse practically eliminated State lines, that the need for such harmonization was made apparent. In 1884 the first attempt to give Congress power to make uniform marriage and divorce laws was made. Since then 59 amendments with this object in view have been pro-

[28] Maynard *v.* Hill, 125 U. S. 190.

[29] Cong. Rec., Feb. 3, 1892, p. 790, Mr. Kyle in re S. R. 29.

posed.[30] While it is assumed that with Congress legislating on the subjects of marriage and divorce the States would not pass individual laws covering the same field, three of these amendments included the provision that the jurisdiction of the Federal Government would be exclusive in this respect.[31]

The supporters of an amendment of this nature claim that the framers of the Constitution omitted such a provision therefrom, as they did not contemplate that such a diversity of statutes on the subject of marriage and divorce as are now found would ever come to pass. They point out that this diversity of laws causes a constant tide of emigration from one State to another by persons seeking to evade the obligation of the marriage relation and the divorce laws of their own States. Further, that as some States do not recognize the divorces granted in others, when such divorces are procured without both parties to the suit being present, it is possible for a man to die leaving two or more lawful wives (lawful in the State where they respectively reside) with two or more lawful sets of children, with all the unfortunate complications caused by the interested parties litigating for the property he may have left in two or more jurisdictions. It is also declared that there is but very little hope that the States independently will come to some harmony on the subject.[32]

So far, however, the action of the committees to which these resolutions have been referred offers hardly any en-

[30] Ames, p. 190. App., Nos. 3, 34, 69, 78, 82, 149, 172, 185, 216, 218, 269, 273, 278, 282, 288, 303, 314, 321, 331, 345, 364, 372, 406, 427, 446, 455, 456, 512, 721, 804, 837, 911, 914, 930, 940, 998, 1000, 1002, 1037, 1058, 1138, 1139, 1149, 1151, 1166, 1176, 1220, 1224, 1268, 1279, 1280, 1285, 1319, 1338, 1345.

[31] App., Nos. 149, 185, 216.

[32] H. Rept. No. 1290, 52d Cong., 1st sess., p. 3.

couragement to the passage of such an amendment. In most cases they have failed to report at all on the resolutions, and in seven cases have definitely declared their objection to the passage of any such legislation.[33] They declare that Congress has too much work already, and that such an amendment would be extended by construction to include the regulation of inheritances and descent of property. Further, that the incorporation of this amendment into the Constitution would work an encroachment upon the rights and duties of the States unfavorable to the idea of their sovereignty clearly guaranteed by the Constitution. With regard to individual State recognition or nonrecognition of divorces of other States, they assert that Congress already has power, under Article IV, section 1, of the Constitution to prescribe the effect to be given in any State to divorces granted in other States. "Why may not Congress by a general statute prescribe that a judgment or decree of divorce shall be valid in every State only when duly proven to have been obtained bona fide on proof of a legal ground and after personal service of the defendant?" [34]

37. Divorces.

The alarming increase in the number of divorces granted in this country has led to the consideration of such drastic action as the universal prohibition of divorce with the right to remarry. On February 4, 1914, in a speech on this subject, Senator Ransdell, of Louisiana, declared that with statistics showing in 1887 1 divorce for every 17 marriages, and in 1906 1 for every 12 marriages, if the divorces multi-

[33] Ames, p. 190, footnote 1. App., Nos. 69, 78, 273, 278, 288, 427.

[34] H. Rept. No. 1290, 52d Cong., 1st sess., accompanying H. J. Res. No. 46.

ply at the same rate, " and there is every indication that they will increase faster, we will have in 1946 the appalling figure of 1 divorce for every 5 marriages. " This, he ascribed to the ease with which divorces, except in a very few jurisdictions, could be procured in the various States.

He recommended, therefore, the passage of a constitutional amendment prohibiting absolute divorce with the right to remarry, and providing for the passage of uniform laws with regard to marriage and to separation from bed and board without permission to remarry.[35]

The remedy suggested by Senator Ransdell, prompted, as he said, because "the malady is so fatal that nothing short of it will prove efficacious," has not been indorsed by many other legislators, but movements in the direction of curbing the divorce evil have been numerous. In 1911, Mr. Volstead, of Minnesota, introduced two amendments covering this field. One provided that Congress should define and limit the causes for divorce, permitting the States to impose restrictions in addition to those imposed by Congress, and the other declaring that "no divorce shall be granted in any State except under and as authorized by its laws, which may permit or prohibit divorces for any and all causes therefor defined by Congress." [36] In 1918 he reintroduced this amendment.[37]

Probably in an effort to induce other States to follow the example of South Carolina in forbidding absolute divorce, 13 proposals have been made for an amendment declaring that the respective States of the Union shall have the right to abolish divorces entirely.[38] Two of

[35] Cong. Rec., Feb. 4, 1914, p. 2863. App., No. 744.

[36] App., Nos. 842, 843.

[37] App., No. 941.

[38] App., Nos. 837, 838, 911, 914, 930, 998, 1000, 1002, 1037, 1058, 1151, 1166, 1224.

these provided that the absolute prohibition could come about only through a majority popular vote to that effect.[39]

An amendment introduced by Mr. Emerson, of Ohio, in 1916 provided that Congress should have power to pass laws regulating divorce and providing for the maintenance of the involved children and the fixing of alimony.[40]

38. Miscegenation.

The effective prohibition by State legislation of mixed marriages has made a constitutional amendment to this effect unnecessary, but three such proposals have been made. The first one in 1871 was probably based upon the erroneous supposition that the fourteenth amendment deprived States of the power to prohibit the intermarriage of persons of the white and colored races.[41] The second, introduced in 1912 by Mr. Roddenberg, of Georgia, was intended to clearly define the prohibition of intermarriage between negroes or persons of color with other races by stating that the phrase "persons of color" is "here employed to mean any and all persons of African descent or having any trace of African, or negro, blood." [42] On January 5, 1928, Senator Blease, of South Carolina, submitted an amendment declaring that the marriage of white persons with negroes or mulattoes shall be void, and providing for the punishment of the parties attempting to contract or perform such marriages.[43]

[39] App., Nos. 838, 914.

[40] App., No. 831.

[41] Ames, p. 190.

[42] App., No. 660.

[43] App., No. 1342.

39. Money.

That the extent and limitation on the power of Congress to issue money for the purpose of legal tender are not definitely fixed was well illustrated by the famous "Legal Tender cases."

Within two years two decisions diametrically opposed to each other in effect were rendered by the Supreme Court—Hepburn *v.* Griswold [44] declaring the legal tender acts unconstitutional and Parker *v.* Davis [45] declaring them constitutional. The latter of these decisions was based mainly on the ground of expediency, so that the business of the country might not suffer, as it undoubtedly would have suffered had the paper money been declared invalid for debts which had been incurred prior to the passage of this legislation. Later on, however, in 1884, in Julliard *v.* Greenbaum,[46] the right of Congress to make paper currency a legal tender was declared one of its permanent powers derived from the States and that such power could be exercised in times of peace as well as in war. It went further and declared that the question as to whether a sufficient urgency had arisen for the issuance of paper money was a "political question to be determined by Congress when the question of exigency arises, and not a judicial question to be afterwards passed upon by the courts."

This last decision, it is claimed by some legislators, gives Congress too much latitude in the matter of money, and that an amendment to the Constitution should specifically

---

[44] 8 Wall. 603.

[45] 12 Wall. 457.

[46] 110 U. S. 421.

enumerate the powers of Congress in this respect. Furthermore, that the currency of the United States is too complicated and should be simplified.[47] Most of all, such an amendment is needed to definitely and conclusively fix the legality and negotiability of Government money for all purposes, so that a change in personnel of the Supreme Court may not bring about conflicting decisions, as happened in the "Legal-Tender cases."

One amendment designed to bring about all these reforms was introduced by Mr. Bowers, of California, in 1892, and provided that—

> A national currency circulating medium shall be issued to the amount of $20 per capita. Said currency, with gold and silver coin of these United States of present weight and fineness, the dollar being the standard or unit of values, and such currency as may be issued in lieu of gold or silver coin, or bullion held exclusively for exchange for currency, shall constitute the only legal money of these United States; and shall be received at par in satisfaction of all obligations for the payment of money within the jurisdiction of these United States.[48]

This amendment was unfavorably reported on by the Committee on the Judiciary to which it had been referred, but the minority in an able and extended report declared their faith in the proposed legislation and stated that there were five important reasons why it should pass:

First. It provided for a simple currency system which would be easily understood by the people as opposed to the present complicated system.

[47] There are at present gold-coin currency, silver-dollar currency, fractional-silver currency, gold-certificate currency, silver-certificate currency, national-bank currency, treasury-note currency under law of 1890. (H. Rept. No. 2614, 52d Cong., 1st sess.)

[48] App., No. 102.

Second. It would make the currency as nearly uniform as possible, and it would make the three elements—gold, silver, and paper—equal in value so that discrimination would cease.

Third. It would put the currency that measures the value of the property of the citizens beyond the reach of the annual disturbance by legislation.

Fourth. It would put the currency on such a firm basis that banks and trust companies could not threaten and produce panics.

Fifth. It would constitute a permanent currency, sufficient in amount, uniform in value, sufficiently flexible and one that would command the confidence of the people.[49]

This amendment was introduced once before, but was not reported.[50] The first amendment on this subject was introduced by Mr. White, of Ohio, in 1892, and it was also unfavorably reported. It provided for Congress to have sole power to coin and issue money and regulate its value. Also, " that all money coined or issued shall be a full legal tender in payment of all debts, public and private, any contract to the contrary notwithstanding." [51]

40. Export duties.

The Constitution directly prohibits Congress from laying any tax or duty on exports (Art. I, sec. 9, cl. 5) and practically denies the States the same power by declaring that " no State shall, without the consent of Congress, lay any imposts or duties on imports or exports." (Art. I,

[49] H. Rept. No. 2614, 52d Cong., 1st sess., p. 8.
[50] App., No. 101 by Mr. Felton, of California, Apr. 19, 1892.
[51] App., No. 77.

sec. 10, cl. 2.) The term "exports" in these provisions has been interpreted by the Supreme Court to refer to goods exported to foreign countries.[52] This prohibition was undoubtedly intended to protect the agricultural States from burdensome taxation, and only 12 attempts have been made since the adoption of the Constitution to abolish the ban.[53] These amendments have been introduced in three groups, and with but one exception (that proposed in 1884) were all prompted by conditions of war. The financial embarrassments of the country during the War of 1812 and the War of the Rebellion suggested to certain legislators the feasibility of assisting the Treasury by removing the prohibition of taxes on exports; and the sudden drop in the quantity of imports occasioned by the World War in 1914 led to the attempt to make up on exports the deficit in revenue resulting from the decrease in imports.

41. Import duties.

The tariff measure of 1907, commonly referred to as the Payne-Aldrich bill, gave the President power to appoint a tariff board to assist in the determination of the exact duties to be levied under the act. Contrary to the wishes of many who desired that the board should have the power to initiate inquests and investigations as a basis for future tariff legislation, its duties were confined to recommendations to the Executive on the application of the maximum and minimum rates specifically set out in the law.[54]

---

[52] Willoughby, Constitution of the United States, p. 221.

[53] Ames, pp. 246–247. App., Nos. 574, 764, 765.

[54] Ogg, F. A. National Progress, p. 36.

Of course, without a constitutional amendment, Congress could not confer upon this tariff board or any other such commission plenary powers in the making up of tariff rates, as this is a duty assigned to Congress by Article I, section 8, clause 2, of the Constitution. Two attempts have thus far been made to authorize Congress to delegate its powers in this respect. One was introduced by Mr. Neely, of West Virginia, in 1916, and declared that "Congress shall have power to confer upon a commission or board power to establish and modify rates of duties and imposts on imports.[55] The other was submitted the next year by Mr. Church, of California, and was intended to take the question of tariff entirely out of politics by providing that "Congress shall have power to lay and collect taxes, duties, imposts, and excises, except duties on goods and commodities imported into this country over which the United States Tariff Commission shall have exclusive jurisdiction."[56]

In 1922, Mr. Ansorge, of New York, proposed an amendment providing for the creation of a permanent tariff board of nine members, not more than five of which to be members of the same political party, the members to hold office for life. The members of this board were to be appointed by the President with the advice and consent of the Senate. The amendment was referred to the Committee on Ways and Means but was never reported out.[57]

Some political writers observe that it is hardly to be expected that Congress will ever seriously contemplate the

[55]App., No. 840.
[56]App., No. 875.
[57]App., No. 1120.

relinquishment in any great degree of its greatest strength as a legislative body—that of providing revenue through the adjustment of tariff duties. It would be quite consistent with legislative efficiency, however, for it to depend for its material of information upon trained tariff experts, and a definite move was made in this direction by the act of Congress approved September 8, 1916, creating the United States Tariff Commission.[58] This commission has authority to investigate the administration, operation, and effects of the customs laws and their relation to the Federal revenue, and to report to the President, the Ways and Means Committee of the House of Representatives, and Finance Committee of the Senate such information as may be called for in this field.[59]

42. Trusts and monopolies.

The last quarter of the nineteenth century witnessed a development and extension of corporate enterprise in the United States never before experienced in this country or elsewhere. Under the many advantages of large production in decreased cost of manufacture, corporations gradually displaced almost entirely individual or partnership undertakings. This trend in big-scale production went further: If a corporation had the advantage over private individuals in the matter of economy in manufacture and administration, a number of corporations amalgamated together could proportionally make still greater profits than the single corporation. There accordingly grew up the great combinations of trade which became one of the

[58] Bernhardt, Joshua. The Tariff Commission, pp. 14–18.
[59] Ibid., pp. 24–38.

most important topics of public discussion upon the ushering in of the twentieth century.[60]

The stifling of competition brought about by these huge combinations, with the concomitant monopolitic control over the selling price of their various commodities, created a fear on the part of some of the American people that such monopolies were dangerous to the free institutions of America. The attempted investigation of the Standard Oil Co. by the Legislature of Ohio in 1886 increased the alarm that there was something sinister in the activities of all such trusts. (It was charged that Senator Payne had been elected to the Senate by the Legislature of Ohio through bribes given by the Standard Oil Co.)[61]

Under the insistent demand that something be done to curb the declared growing influence of trusts and monopolies, Congress in 1888 proceeded to a consideration of feasible control and restraint of such combinations. They were met at the outset by the constitutional limitation that the Federal Government can not intervene in the business of corporations created by State charter, but after a discussion of two years a law was agreed to which was assumed to be constitutional under the interstate-commerce clause. (Art. I, sec. 8, cl. 3.) This law, commonly known as the Sherman Antitrust Act, provided that combinations and conspiracies in restraint of trade among the several States and with foreign countries were illegal and punishable by fine or imprisonment.[62]

---

[60] Hendrick, Burton J. Age of Big Business, pp. 1–58.

[61] Tarbell, Ida. History of the Standard Oil Co. Vol. II, ch. 13, the Standard Oil Co. and Politics, pp. 111–128.

[62] Dewey, Davis Rich. National Problems, p. 198, citing U. S. Statutes, 51st Cong., 1st sess., ch. dcxlvii.

This legislation, however, failed to meet the demands made of it. During Harrison's administration, seven out of eight decisions rendered by the Federal courts under this law were adverse to the Government.[63] In the well-known Knight case[64] the Supreme Court declared that the power to regulate interstate commerce does not include any power over commerce within a State and has no direct relation, in the sense of the Constitution, to production or manufacture, and does not include any power to repress or control combinations or conspiracies, or monopoly in the production or manufacture or in the sale of the product. The opinion delivered in the case of Addyston Pipe & Steel Co. *v.* United States[65] further confirmed the inability of Congress to reach those monopolistic firms which, although doing business all over the United States, maintained factories in the same States where the products were sold.[66]

In the endeavor to give Congress the plainly needed authority to go into the States if the Federal Government was to be expected to accomplish anything in repressing trusts, Mr. Jenkins, of Wisconsin, introduced a measure intended to furnish Congress with the necessary constitutional grant. His resolution (H. J. Res. 138)[67] was referred to the House Judiciary Committee and by them exchanged for House Joint Resolution 174 submitted by Mr. Ray, of New York. The latter proposition was favorably reported to the House on May 15, 1900, and declared that "Congress shall have power to define, regu-

[63] Dewey, Davis Rich. National Problems, pp. 201–202.
[64] 156 U. S. 1.
[65] 175 U. S. 211.
[66] Thompson, Merle. Trust Dissolution, pp. 36–38.
[67] App., No. 296.

late, prohibit, or dissolve trusts, monopolies, or combinations whether existing in the form of a corporation or otherwise." [68]

The report accompanying this resolution strongly urged the passage of the amendment, saying that under the decisions of the Supreme Court on the subject a constitutional amendment was indispensable to give Congress power to control and repress undesirable combinations of trade; that the States were powerless to enact any laws operative outside their respective territorial limits; and that on account of the great variety in the State incorporation laws, corporations denied business activity in one State could easily go into some other State where the laws were not so strict; and further that " no State can exclude from its territory the corporation of another State engaged in interstate commerce, and hence a monopoly in manufacture existing in one State, if also engaged in interstate commerce, may, so far as any State is concerned, carry its product into every State and control the price and market everywhere." [69]

While practically the entire House membership was in favor of Federal control over trusts and monopolies, the passage of the amendment was made impossible by the inclusion of a section which read: " The several States may continue to exercise such power in any manner not in conflict with the laws of the United States." It was openly charged by the Democrats, in the consideration of this measure, that the Republicans had purposely worded the resolution so as to make the States subservient to Congress, knowing full well that the requisite ratification of

[68] App., No. 306.

[69] H. Rept. No. 1501, 56th Cong., 1st sess.

three-fourths of the States, by reason of that provision could never be secured.

The Democrats regarded the Ray proposition not only as a scheme to postpone, perhaps indefinitely, all governmental action against the trusts and incidentally to entrap the Democrats into withdrawing the issue of the campaign of 1900 but also in case the amendment should be finally adopted as an abridgment of the rights and powers of the States.

The Republicans were accused of espousing the cause of the trusts and that this amendment was proposed to allay suspicion, feeling quite confident it would never pass.[70]

The passage of the amendment was also opposed by some on the ground that Congress already had sufficient power to control trusts, and that it was merely necessary to amend the Sherman Act in accordance with the suggestions made by the courts in construing it.[71] A bill providing for such amendment was already before the House, and many Members gave notice that while they would vote against the adoption of the constitutional amendment they would vote affirmatively to amend the Sherman law. The constitutional amendment came to a vote June 1 and failed to receive the necessary two-thirds affirmative vote, the count being 154 yeas to 132 nays.[72]

On the next day the vote was taken on the bill (H. R. 10539) providing for broadening the Sherman law so as to make it more comprehensive and increasing the penal-

[70] Editorial in Washington Post May 31, 1900, quoted by Mr. Richardson, Cong. Rec., May 31, 1900, p. 6300.

[71] Cong. Rec., May 31, 1900, p. 6323.

[72] Cong. Rec., June 1, 1900, p. 6426.

ties for the infraction thereof. It was passed by a practical unanimity of 274 to 1.[73]

That the existence and activities of monopolies and trusts was at this time quite generally considered to be a serious problem is illustrated by the fact that no fewer than 18 amendments giving Congress power for their regulation and suppression were introduced from 1899 to 1913.[74]

It has now, however, been pretty generally assumed that such power as is consistent with the spirit of our system of dual government is already contained in the original grant to Congress, and that no amendment is necessary or desirable giving the Federal Government a greater control over corporations.

43. Protection of trade-marks.

It was originally thought that Congress had the power under Article I, section 8, clause 8, of the Constitution to grant exclusive rights to originators of trade-marks, but it was decided in the Trade-Mark cases [75] that trade-marks have no necessary relation to invention or discovery which bring them within that provision. The only source of power over such trade-marks would be in the interstate clause (Art. I, sec. 8, cl. 3), and, acting under that authority, Congress, in 1881, passed a law protecting trade-marks used in commerce between States, foreign nations,

[73] Cong. Rec., June 2, 1900, p. 6501. This bill failed to come to a vote in the Senate. (Cong. Rec., Mar. 2, 1901, p. 3439.)

[74] App., Nos. 19, 39, 86, 152, 283, 296, 301, 306, 310, 337, 355, 363, 373, 391, 572, 586, 730.

[75] 100 U. S., 82.

and the Indian tribes. This law of course could have no application to trade-marks used exclusively within the confines of a particular State. Four amendments have accordingly been introduced in the attempt to give Congress the power to grant, protect, and regulate the exclusive right to adopt and use trade-marks.[76] The last two of these amendments also give Congress the power to negotiate international treaties on this subject.

44. The treaty-making power.

Although the House of Representatives does not participate in the actual ratification of treaties negotiated by the President, its consent to the provisions thereof is always necessary on account of its joint responsibility with the Senate in appropriating the necessary funds to carry it into effect.[77] The question has frequently arisen as to whether the House could prevent a treaty from going into effect by refusing the necessary appropriation. On March 24, 1796, the House of Representatives, believing that it had this power, called on the President for certain facts relating to the Jay treaty. President Washington declined to comply with the request, declaring that the Constitution put the treaty-making power exclusively in the hands of the President and Senate, and once they had concurred it was the duty of the House to acquiesce.[78] This interpretation prompted the Legislature of Virginia to recommend an amendment providing that any treaty which had provisions affecting the powers of Congress should not become the supreme law of the land until it had been approved by a majority of the House of Repre-

[76] App., Nos. 619, 684; Ames, p. 266.

[77] Mathews, John M. The Conduct of Foreign Relations, p. 201.

[78] Moore's International Digest, vol. 5, pp. 224–225.

sentatives. Two amendments of a similar nature were introduced in 1884 and in 1885.[79]

No further efforts were made in this direction until 1919, when the delay of the Senate in reaching a vote on the Versailles treaty prompted Mr. Griffin, of New York, to present a resolution declaring that all treaties shall be ratified by a majority vote of both the House of Representatives and Senate.[80] This resolution was reintroduced by Mr. Griffin in 1921, 1923, 1925, and in 1927.[81]

A constitutional amendment providing for the House approval of treaties would be entirely consistent with our system of government as at present constituted. It is obliged to consider the provisions of all treaties in order that they may be brought into full effect through the proper appropriations, and it has been held that a treaty which affects commercial arrangements with foreign powers already attended to by statute can not operate to modify such arrangements until the assent of Congress has been obtained.[82] It is also recognized that the House may by resolution concur with the Senate in initiating treaties by calling upon the President to negotiate with other countries regarding certain international questions,[83] and the Senate acknowledges that when the provisions of any contemplated treaty in any way involve revenue laws (the origin of which must always occur in the House of Representatives) a clause must be inserted declaring that such provisions are dependent upon the action of Congress.[84]

---

[79]Ames, p. 268.
[80]App., No. 1003.
[81]App., Nos. 1040, 1160, 1264, 1324.
[82] Willoughby. Constitutional Law of the United States, p. 166.
[83] Ibid., p. 158.
[84] Ibid., p. 167.

The agitation in America and other neutral countries during the first year or two of the World War for the founding of some international tribunal competent to efficiently settle differences between contending nations led to the presentation in 1916 by Senator Shafroth, of Colorado, of an amendment authorizing the President, with the consent of two-thirds of both Houses of Congress, to negotiate and conclude a treaty with the other nations, providing for the establishment of an international tribunal with power to bind all the signatory powers to an execution of all obligations thereunder and an obedience to the decisions of the court.[85] This resolution never got beyond the preliminary stage.

TERMINATION OF WAR

The possibilities of an indefinite delay in the termination of a war status, illustrated by the controversy which arose in the Senate over the provisions of the treaty negotiated with Spain at the conclusion of the Cuban war,[86] led Mr. Grow, of Pennsylvania, to introduce an amendment providing that as Commander in Chief of the Army and Navy the President had the authority to negotiate a treaty ending a war, and that a majority of the Senate was sufficient to ratify treaties.[87] The apprehension of Mr. Grow in 1899 that under our present system of ratifying

[85] App., No. 845.

[86] A fierce debate arose over the annexation of the Philippines, and it was only the conciliatory attitude of Mr. Bryan's followers and the breaking out of the insurrection in those islands which brought the treaty to a vote. Latane, John Holladay. America as a World Power, p. 77.

[87] Mathews, John M. The Conduct of American Foreign Relations, Ch. XVII; The Termination of War, pp. 319, 341. App., No. 250.

treaties the termination of a state of war might be indefinitely delayed, bore fruition in 1919–20 when the United States continued in a state of war for over two years after the termination of hostilities on account of the inability of the proponents of the Versailles treaty to muster a two-thirds senatorial vote in its favor.[88] This treaty would easily have passed the Senate if only a majority vote were required by the Constitution, and in order to make the passage of future treaties an easier matter Senator Owen, of Oklahoma, proposed in 1920 an amendment stipulating that a favorable vote of a majority of the Senators present would be sufficient to ratify any treaty.[89] Senator Owen repeated this resolution in 1921 and 1923.[90]

During the discussion of the Versailles treaty, with its League of Nations, much was said about supergovernment and the relinquishment of sovereign rights. It was such discussion which actuated the introduction by Mr. Newton, of Missouri, of the following amendment: [91]

> All treaties which affect the sovereignty of the United States, the territorial boundaries thereof, impair the rights of any State to its local self-government, directly or indirectly amend the Constitution, or which will result in lowering the Stars and Stripes, the flag of our country, to be supplanted by an international flag, or any other flag, shall not become effective unless same have been submitted at a general or special election by a majority of the qualified voters of the United States voting upon the proposition.

---

[88] Mathews, Conduct of American Foreign Relations, pp. 328–329.

[89] The difficulties experienced with the Versailles treaty must not be taken as a criterion of all treaty ratification. The fact that 595 treaties were successfully ratified from 1889 to 1914 would indicate that the Senate is usually in accord with the President on treaties negotiated by him. Quincy Wright on the Control of American Foreign Relations, pp. 246–477. App., No. 1017.

[90] App., Nos. 1054, 1190.

[91] App., No. 1031.

45. War powers.

The constitutional ratifying conventions of New York and Rhode Island proposed that an amendment should be added to the Constitution restricting the power of declaration of war to the concurrence of two-thirds of both Houses of Congress. In 1815 the Hartford convention recommended the same amendment excepting cases where the United States was actually invaded.[92] The history of the United States from that year to the outbreak of the World War has evidently been such as to allay the fear that our legislators might, through the influences of private interests or war hysteria, declare for an unpopular war, since during this long period not a single amendment was proposed restricting the war powers of Congress. Commencing with 1914, however, there have been 17 resolutions introduced designed to restrict Congress in its power to declare war.

These amendments were prompted by the epidemic of wars throughout the world during this period and the few years immediately preceding, and the feeling that since there was by no means a unanimity of opinion among the people in favor of war, they should be given the opportunity to determine for themselves if the Nation should initiate hostilities.

Accordingly 14 of these resolutions declared that Congress could declare war only in the event of an imminent peril such as invasion or insurrection, or after a majority of the people voting on such measure had declared in favor of war.[93] Three of these amendments contained the

[92]Ames, p. 269.

[93]App., Nos. 776, 798, 829, 927, 962, 1178, 1080, 1111, 1213, 1228, 1286, 1294, 1313, 1363.

interesting provision that the President and Senate were to be given power to negotiate treaties with other nations to the effect that war would not be declared between the United States and any one of these nations until a favorable vote on hostilities had been cast by the electors of the country proposing war.[94]

The first amendment of this series was introduced by Mr. Bartholdt, of Missouri, on July 21, 1914, and was designed to keep the United States out of all overseas war by prohibiting Congress from declaring war except to repel invasion or under circumstances calling for measures of self-defense.[95]

An amendment introduced in 1924 by Mr. Thomas, of Oklahoma, provided that Congress could declare war only upon the concurrence of three-fourths of the elected members.[96] One proposed by Senator Frazier, of North Dakota, in April, 1926, and again in December, 1927, purported to declare for the complete abolition of war.[97]

The enormous profits made by corporations and business men during the Great War has led to the introduction in Congress of eight amendments providing that in time of war Congress shall declare for conscription of not only men but " of all money, industries, and property of whatsoever nature necessary to the prosecution thereof, and shall limit the profits for the use of such money, industries, and property." [98] Two of these amendments give Congress the further power to stabilize prices of services and commodities deemed essential during war time.[99]

---

[94] App., Nos. 927, 1080, 1178.
[95] App., No. 760.
[96] App., No. 1245.
[97] App., No. 1293.
[98] App., Nos. 1122, 1195, 1200, 1246, 1258, 1277, 1314, 1315.
[99] App., Nos. 1277, 1315.

One of the active champions of this cause in the House of Representatives has been Mr. Johnson, of South Dakota, who, in addition to submitting two joint resolutions, introduced a bill (H. R. 4841) covering the same subject. When questioned by Mr. Hull, of Iowa, as to the constitutionality of such legislation Mr. Johnson replied that he did not doubt the House could anticipate the war powers given to Congress even when there was no war. "At least," said Mr. Johnson, "we have laid down the rule and no one can test the constitutionality except in time of war, and if it is then tested Congress could speedily reenact the law and there would be no profiteering."[1]

While there is a fair preponderance of opinion that industry and capital should be made to bear their share of the burdens of war, it is apparent that legislation or a constitutional amendment bringing this about is a very difficult thing to frame and do justice to all. Mr. McSwain, of South Carolina, in discussing the proposition, declared that a commission should be appointed to thoroughly study the question and report to Congress.[2]

Another amendment in this field was that introduced by Mr. Wolff, of Missouri, providing that all those owing allegiance to the United States who, during war time, defraud the Government in respect of war materials, shall be guilty of treason.[3]

46. The Army.

To avoid any possibility of the United States becoming a militaristic nation, seven of the ratifying conventions recommended the passage of amendments designed to

---

[1] Cong. Rec., vol. 66, pt. 3, Jan. 30, 1925, pp. 2370–2731.

[2] Ibid., p. 2734.

[3] App., No. 1237.

prevent the supporting of a large army except in time of war. Two attempts to accomplish this same end were also made in the First Congress.[4] A prohibition of this nature in the Constitution is hardly necessary, as there is but little desire in this country for large standing armies, and clause 12 of section 8 of Article I of the Constitution, which prevents appropriations for the Army for a period longer than two years, quite effectually keeps the military under the control of the people.

The only other amendment pertaining to the Army came in 1919, when Mr. James, of Michigan, presented a resolution forbidding Congress to conscript armies for foreign service to execute orders of any international body.[5] This amendment was prompted by the possibility of the United States entering the League of Nations, whose constitution was interpreted as putting each signatory power thereto under contribution for troops in the event of trouble.

An amendment was introduced by Mr. Miller, of Wisconsin (by request), in 1893, which declared, among other impractical things, that the Army and Navy should be abolished and that the militia of the several States should be under the call of the President for executing the laws of the Union.[6]

47. The militia.

Outside of the recommendations made by three of the ratifying conventions (that the States should entirely control the militia when Congress failed to act, that the militia should not be subject to martial law except when in

[4]Ames, p. 270.
[5]App., No. 1004.
[6]App., No. 114.

actual service, and that the militia should not be called for service outside its State for a period longer than six weeks without the consent of the legislature, none of which were accepted by Congress), only two other efforts were made during the first century of American constitutional history to change the constitutional power of Congress over the militia. These came in 1817 and 1818, when General Harrison, of Ohio, urged that Congress, concurrently with the States, should provide for the training of the militia. These amendments were suggested by the ineffectual work of the militia during the War of 1812.[7]

Practically another hundred years elapsed before Congress was again called to consider constitutional amendments concerning the militia. This came in 1916, when three amendments were introduced within a week's time (January 24–31) designed to give the Federal Government a bigger control over the State militia. Generally they provided that Congress should have the power to call the militia for training and drilling, to execute the laws of the Nation, suppress insurrections, and repel invasions.[8] One of them provided also for amending Article III, section 2, of the Constitution so as to make the President Commander in Chief of the Army, Navy, and militia.[9] Another declared that the militia should be subject to duty within and without the United States.[10]

These amendments were prompted by the disordered conditions on the Mexican border, which could at any time develop into cause for national military action, and the

[7]Ames., pp. 270–271.
[8]App., Nos. 824, 825, 828.
[9]App., No. 824.
[10]App., No. 825.

recognized unpreparedness of the State militia to efficiently cope with such a situation. That the militia was in fact unprepared was well demonstrated when it was sent to the border by President Wilson and it developed that almost two-thirds of the militiamen were practically without military training and, owing to the divided Federal and State control, three months elapsed before the fields units could receive the proper equipment for action.[11]

On June 3, 1916, Congress passed the national defense act, which included within its provisions measures for the better control and guidance by the War Department of the State militia and thus designed to prevent a recurrence of the deficiencies in the militia as demonstrated in the Mexican campaign.[12] This law was criticized by military experts, who declared that while federalization was carried so far that some of its provisions were of doubtful constitutionality they would not give better results.[13]

48. Military pensions.

The universal conviction that men who have given their services to their country in time of war should be assisted by the Government in their days of dependency, due to wounds, illness, or old age, has kept the Constitution free from any limitation on Congress to grant pensions.[14] For over 100 years not a limiting amendment of this nature was suggested. In fact, the only amendment on this subject during the first century was in the other

[11] Ogg, F. A. National Progress, p. 300.

[12] Ibid., p. 387, citing 39 U. S. Stat. L., Pt. I, pp. 166–217.

[13] Ibid., p. 388.

[14] Glasson, Wm. H. Federal Military Pensions in the United States, pp. 1–5.

direction and provided that general pension laws should not be repealed, nor should a rate of pension granted under same be decreased.[15]

During the last decade of the nineteenth century, however, a movement took hold to check the enormous flow of Government funds into pension channels. The practical leader of this movement was President Cleveland, who vetoed special and general pension bills to an extent never known before or since.[16] His opposition to these pension measures was not due to any unfriendliness for the soldier, but to the conviction that pensions should be granted only in designated meritorious cases and not blindly to all who had worn a uniform, irrespective as to the nature of service.[17]

It is sometimes claimed that the activity of many a legislator for a certain pension law is due to a desire to increase his political prestige among his ex-soldier constituency, irrespective as to the national policy on such measures.

To suppress this alleged source of agitation for private pension laws, and at the same time to limit and restrict Congress in its power to grant general pensions, Mr. Hayes, of Iowa, in 1892 introduced an amendment declaring that—

> No pension, nor any pay or emolument, that does not cease in the actual service shall hereafter be granted, allowed, or paid to or on account of any soldier or sailor, except under the provisions of law existing at the time of enlistment, nor unless claimed within two years from time right to same accrues under law.[18]

---

[15] Ames, p. 271.

[16] Glasson, Federal Military Pensions, Ch. III, Pensions and Politics, pp. 204–274. Mason, Veto Power, p. 165.

[17] Dewey, National Problems, pp. 82–88.

[18] App., No. 104.

This would provide for a systematic payment of pensions based on service and sacrifice, because as the law would have to be passed before the military service was rendered there would be no need or desire for a legislator to advocate pension measures for merely political reasons as he would not know the status of any future constituency.

Mr. Hayes again introduced this amendment in 1893, but neither one was reported on by the committee to which referred.[19] In 1898 Mr. Clark, of Iowa, submitted an amendment proposing to restrict the payment of pensions after July 1, 1898, to only such soldiers and sailors as were discharged with a wound or disability and to widows, minor children, and dependent mothers of deceased service men.[20]

The amendment referred to in section 46 regarding the Army also contained a provision abolishing the present pension system and declaring that all pensions shall be paid by the counties.[21]

49. Prohibition of polygamy.

In 1875 the first amendment declaring for the prohibition of polygamy in the United States was introduced in Congress. Since then 53 such amendments have been presented.[22]

The agitation for this amendment was based practically entirely on the practice of polygamy by the Mormons in

[19]App., No. 119.

[20]App., No. 237.

[21]App., No. 114.

[22]Ames, p. 272; App., Nos. 3, 20, 88, 251, 252, 254, 270, 286, 290, 304, 295, 335, 347, 377, 380, 381, 410, 443, 481, 495, 502, 638, 715, 724, 736, 738, 742, 743, 784, 929, 949, 997, 1072, 1073, 1221.

Utah (and somewhat in Idaho). In 1882 Congress attempted to stamp out polygamy in Utah by taking away the suffrage, as well as the right to hold office, from any person guilty of cohabitation with more than one wife.[23] Congress also declared that Utah could not hope for admission to the Union as a State until she effectually banned polygamous conduct within her borders. President Harrison in 1891 recommended to Congress that Utah should not be made a State until she had given "satisfactory evidence" that after admission she would "make, enforce, and maintain" effective laws against polygamy.[24] The difficulty lay in the fact that even though the Utah Territory should declare that after its admission to the Union it would enforce laws prohibiting polygamy there was no way of compelling obedience to such guaranty should the Utah State refuse to punish polygamists.

It was therefore felt that the only true effective way to destroy the evil of polygamy in Utah was to declare its ban throughout the United States by a constitutional amendment. Mr. Bushnell, of Wisconsin, particularly urged this method of settling the vexed question in urging the adoption of his amendment in 1892.[25] No action was taken on his amendment, and as Utah was made a State in 1895 under circumstances and with assurances indicating a definite abandonment of the practice of polygamy, the matter did not come up for constitutional discussion again until 1899. It was then declared that Utah had broken faith with the pledge made while she was still a

[23] Dewey, National Problems, p. 159, citing U. S. Stat., 47th Cong., 1st sess., ch. xlvii.

[24] Messages and Papers of Presidents, Vol. XIII, p. 5641.

[25] App., No. 88.

Territory by permitting the election in 1888 of Brigham H. Roberts, an "avowed polygamist," to Congress.

An amendment was accordingly introduced February 6, 1899, by Mr. Capron, of Rhode Island, disqualifying all polygamists for Congress and banning polygamy from the land.[26] In the report which accompanied this resolution (H. Res. 354) it was pointed out that since many Mormons still religiously believed there was nothing immoral about polygamy, the passage of the amendment by three-fourths of the States would impress upon them the evil and impurity of the practice. This amendment was never voted upon, but on the 23d of January, 1900, the House of Representatives by resolution (H. Res. 107) declared the seat of the Representative from Utah vacant. He was excluded on a vote of 268 yeas to 50 nays.[27] The vote might have been unanimous except that some of the Representatives opined that since Roberts had been duly elected according to law he should be allowed to take his seat and then later be expelled under Article I, section 5, clause 2, of the Constitution.[28]

On December 4, 1899, Mr. Capron again introduced his amendment, which was referred to the Committee on Election of President, Vice President, and Representatives in Congress, and by them recommended for passage, declaring that "notwithstanding the action of the House in the Roberts case, at best it can only be regarded as a precedent for future guidance of the House only, and that, while it may be persuasive, it can scarcely be held as a binding force and efficiency of a constitutional provision that should control alike and without question or

[26] App., No. 251.

[27] Cong. Rec., Jan. 23, 1900, p. 1217.

[28] H. Rept. No. 85, 56th Cong., 1st sess.

doubt both the House and the Senate, and set forever at rest a question that has been made the subject of such vital concern by the American people." [29]

Despite the unanimity of condemnation of polygamy manifested by the House in the discussion of this resolution, nevertheless serious objections arose to its passage. Some Members declared that the adoption of such an amendment would take away from the States the power to legislate on the offenses connected with adultery, a jurisdiction exclusively within their control, and would set a bad precedent for invading the sovereign rights of the States.[30] This opinion was maintained despite section 4 of this resolution, which declared that "nothing in the Constitution or in this article shall be construed to deny to any State the exclusive power, subject to the provisions of this article, to make and enforce all laws concerning marriage and divorce within its jurisdiction, or to vest in the United States any power respecting the same within any State."

Other Members opposed the adoption of the resolution on the ground that it did not cover a subject of sufficient importance to be incorporated into the Constitution, and that the evil, if any existed, could well be taken care of by the present State and Federal laws.[31] This amendment was eventually recommitted to a committee, this time the Judiciary Committee, and died there.[32]

Two of the thirty-two amendments introduced on this subject since 1889 provided that all persons convicted of having practiced polygamy would be disqualified from

---

[29] H. Rept. No. 348, 56th Cong., 1st sess.

[30] Cong. Rec., Apr. 30, 1900, p. 4862.

[31] Cong. Rec., Apr. 30, 1900, p. 4864.

[32] Cong. Rec., 56th Cong., 1st sess., p. 4861.

holding any office under the United States,[33] and seven of this series enlarged the disqualification to include all State offices.[34] Six of this last series added the provision that such disqualification might be removed by a concurring vote of two-thirds of both Houses of Congress.[35]

50. Protection to labor.

On May 1, 1886, according to more or less prearranged plans engineered by the Knights of Labor, a concerted demand was made by labor throughout the United States for an 8-hour day, and since then the question has regularly been before the country.[36] Efforts to have the respective States pass 8-hour day laws have generally been unsuccessful, and in many States where laws have been passed designating a certain number of hours for certain classes of employment they have been declared unconstitutional as being an arbitrary interference with the freedom of contract.[37]

Efforts to secure the adoption of laws limiting the hours of labor have accordingly been directed toward Congress. It has been maintained by those favoring congressional action in this respect that the difference in number of working hours to the day among the different States works unfair competition and " operates to the disadvantage of both labor and capital in many localities, resulting in unequal earnings for a given amount of capital and unequal wages for a given amount of labor.[38] The number of

[33] App., Nos. 290, 381.

[34] App., Nos. 254, 290, 295, 307, 335, 347, 380.

[35] App., Nos. 290, 304, 295, 307, 335, 347.

[36] Powderly, T. V., Thirty Years of Labor, pp. 471–526.

[37] Department of Labor Bulletin No. 321, pp. 55–69. See particularly Lochner *v.* New York, 198 U. S. 45.

[38] Preamble to H. J. Res. 20, 57th Cong., 1st sess. App., No. 328.

legal working hours per week in the various States range from 58 to 72, a variation which creates conditions of discrimination as between the citizens of the several States.[39]

The only remedy for this condition, they declare, is an amendment to the Federal Constitution granting power to Congress to regulate hours of labor. They feel safe that if Congress is given control over hours of labor it will establish the 8-hour day as the standard.[40] At any rate, labor leaders will find it easier to deal exclusively with one legislature (Congress) than with 48 separate legislatures, and they will thus be able to concentrate their efforts for the 8-hour day, or lower, at one place.

The first amendment in this respect was introduced by Mr. Davis, of Massachusetts, in 1884, and proposed to give Congress power to regulate the hours of labor "which persons may be employed in the manufacture of textile fabrics and in other industries."[41] He reintroduced this amendment in 1886 and 1888.[42] From 1896 to 1913, 14 attempts have been made to amend the Constitution so as to give Congress power to fix the hours of labor,[43] but no one of them has been favorably reported.

An amendment introduced in 1894 by Mr. George, of Mississippi, definitely proposed to make the 8-hour day

[39] Preamble to H. J. Res. 20, 57th Cong., 1st sess. App., No. 328.

[40] Congress has been committed to an 8-hour working day as the standard day's labor in the Government service: Ames, p. 273. Also, Congress in 1916 passed the Adamson law declaring 8 hours the working day on railroads: U. S. Statutes at Large, XXXIX, pt. 1, pp. 721–722.

[41] Ames, p. 273.

[42] Ibid.

[43] App., Nos. 197, 211, 236, 263, 268, 328, 329, 384, 413, 459, 510, 629, 670, 709.

for persons doing manual labor a part of the Constitution.[44]

The last two amendments of this series, both introduced in 1918, went further than any of the others in declaring the control to be exercised by the Federal Government over labor. The first one, which was presented by Mr. Watson, of Pennsylvania, was designed to empower Congress to regulate wages and hours of labor and prices of commodities throughout the United States.[45] The second, submitted by Mr. Dallinger, of Massachusetts, was to give Congress power to regulate the hours and conditions of labor.[46]

51. Child labor.

In 1906 the first bills proposing a Federal child-labor law were introduced in Congress. Nearly 10 years later, September 1, 1916, the first Federal child-labor law was passed. Basing its authority on the power of Congress to regulate interstate and foreign commerce, this act of September 1, 1916, closed the channels of interstate and foreign commerce to the products of child labor.

The day before the act took effect—August 31, 1917—an injunction was granted by the United States District Court for the Western District of North Carolina enjoining the United States attorney of that district from enforcing the act on the ground that it was unconstitutional, and in June, 1918, the Supreme Court of the United States affirmed the decision of this district court in the case of Hammer *v.* Dagenhart.[47]

---

[44]App., No. 151.
[45]App., No. 957.
[46]App., No. 961.
[47] 247 U. S. 251.

Congress then sought to take advantage of another power, that of laying and collecting taxes, and provided for a tax upon the profits of industries employing child labor. This was also declared unconstitutional.[48] In its opinion as to the first law, the Supreme Court was divided 5 to 4; the second was an 8 to 1 decision. The court therefore made the issue clear; either Congress must give up the plan of a Federal minimum and rely solely upon the States, or there must be adopted a Federal amendment definitely giving to Congress the power to pass a child-labor law, since it is plain that under the present Constitution it does not have that power.[49]

This inability on the part of Congress to pass a child-labor law was perhaps foreseen by Mr. Rogers, of Massachusetts, who introduced the first amendment touching the subject of child labor. His resolution was presented in 1914 and was designed to give Congress power to regulate the employment of women and all others under 21 years of age.[50] He reintroduced this same measure in 1918 and again in 1919.[51]

In 1918 Mr. Farr, of Pennsylvania, introduced an amendment conferring upon Congress power to regulate the employment of child labor whose products moved in interstate commerce,[52] and Mr. Mason, of Illinois, introduced an amendment giving Congress authority to prohibit or regulate the employment of all children under

[48] Bailey *v.* Drexel Furniture Co., 42 Sup. Ct. 449 (1922).

[49] 67th Cong., 4th sess., House Rept. No. 1694.

[50] App., No. 759.

[51] App., Nos. 955, 976.

[52] App., No. 956.

16 years of age.[53] Mr. Mason reintroduced his amendment in 1919.[54]

Since then 54 amendments have been proposed providing for Federal regulation and prohibition of child labor. Four of these gave 16 years of age generally and the minimum age for employment.[55] One provided that the labor of children under the age of 16 years in any mine, mill, factory, or workshop shall be prohibited and that Congress shall have power to regulate the employment of persons under 18 years of age engaged in any other employment; [56] two contained the same provisions except that it gave the regulatory powers as of persons over the age of 16 years.[57] Two declared that Congress should have the power to regulate the employment of all persons under the age of 21 years.[58] One attempted to give Congress the power to prohibit the employment of children " under such ages as Congress may from time to time determine," [59] another generally to regulate child labor within all territory of the United States,[60] and one more permitting Congress to prohibit the transportation in interstate commerce of all products of child labor.[61] The other 42 stipulated in varying language that Congress shall have power to regulate the employment and the hours of labor

[53]App., No. 954.
[54]App., No. 992.
[55]App., Nos. 1049, 1225, 1235, 1262.
[56]App., No. 1231.
[57]App., Nos. 1242, 1262.
[58]App., Nos. 1047, 1163.
[59]App., No. 1157.
[60]App., No. 1123.
[61]App., No. 1134.

and conditions of employment of persons under 18 years of age.[62] Twelve of these resolutions included an understanding that power is also reserved to the several States to limit or prohibit child labor in any way which would not lessen any limitation of such labor or prohibition thereof by Congress.

During the fourth session of the Sixty-seventh Congress Mr. Foster, of Ohio, and Senator Shortridge, of California, introduced in the House of Representatives and Senate, respectively, amendments providing that "Congress shall have power concurrent with that of the several States to limit and to prohibit the labor of persons under the age of 18 years." (H. J. Res. 458, S. J. Res. 285.)[63] These were reported on favorably by the House and Senate Committees on the Judiciary, respectively, but did not reach any point of deliberation in the House or Senate.

At the beginning of the Sixty-eighth Congress these two men reintroduced resolutions on the subject, the measures taking the respective titles of House Joint Resolution 184 and Senate Joint Resolution 1. The House resolution being adopted first, it was, when it reached the Senate, substituted for Senate Joint Resolution 1, and under the former title passed the Senate. It read as follows:

SECTION 1. The Congress shall have power to limit, regulate, and prohibit the labor of persons under 18 years of age.

SEC. 2. The power of the several States is unimpaired by this article except that the operation of State laws shall be suspended to the extent necessary to give effect to the legislation enacted by Congress.

---

[62] App., Nos. 1097, 1098, 1099, 1103, 1104, 1105, 1107, 1108, 1110, 1113, 1114, 1115, 1118, 1119, 1128, 1131, 1132, 1135, 1143, 1144, 1145, 1148, 1150, 1152, 1154, 1155, 1159, 1167, 1169, 1174, 1182, 1183, 1185, 1193, 1198, 1202, 1204, 1206, 1210, 1211, 1214, 1238.

[63] App., Nos. 1144, 1145.

After four weeks' hearings and two weeks' deliberation this resolution was reported favorably from the House Committee on the Judiciary by a vote of 15 to 6. The majority report accompanying the resolution declared the total number of working children in the United States (between the ages of 10 and 15 years of age) was 1,060,858, according to the 1920 census. This number was approximately one-twelfth of the total number of children of that age in the entire country. The number of child workers, 10 to 13 years of age, inclusive, was 378,063.

It was submitted by the majority report that the 1920 census, having been taken in January when the Federal child labor tax law was discouraging by a heavy tax the employment of children under 14 in mills and workshops and of children under 16 in mines and quarries, that if taken at present the figure representing the number of child workers would undoubtedly be much greater. It was pointed out that if the proposed amendment were ratified it would not give to Congress a new and untried power, as from the experience had with the two Federal laws, the protection afforded the children and the administrative problems and costs were definitely ascertainable. Further, while this was a new type of Federal legislation, the experience of the Bureau of Chemistry in administering the pure food and drugs act and a series of studies of the administration of the State child labor laws which had been made by the Children's Bureau furnished helpful analogies based on both National and State analogies, which could be effectively used in working out a plan for enforcing National child-labor legislation.[64]

The minority report filed by Mr. Graham, of Pennsylvania, argued strenuously that in opposing the child-labor

[64] 68th Cong., H. Rept. No. 395.

amendment it was not proposed to make any argument against the regulation of child labor.[65] That such regulation is desirous and necessary was admitted, but it was pointed out that the "regulation of child labor is primarily a subject for State legislation and not for national enactment." Further, that already 46 States have enacted regulatory laws, and that while not all of them have risen to the high degree of regulation which the proponents of the resolution deem essential to the welfare of the children, yet there is no valid reason for assuming that "with the use of propaganda, persuasion, and appeal on moral grounds that this enlightened sentiment will not reach the high-water mark of their expectations." One of the reasons given by the proponents of the child-labor amendment was that with different child-labor laws existing in the various States, cost of production varied, thus destroying the possibility of fair competition. To this Mr. Graham replied:

> It is indeed an unbearable suggestion that an amendment to the Constitution should be adopted to control competition. Let that become a basis, and we would soon make that venerable document an undesirable destructive patchwork. Competitive industries with unequal conditions in the several States are numerous and would furnish a basis for many amendments.

The resolution was fully debated in the House and came to a vote on April 26, 1924.[66] Mr. Linthicum, of Maryland, offered an amendment to the effect that ratification not be effected until it had been accepted by conventions specially called in three-fourths of the States and within five years from the submission thereof. The amendment was rejected.[67]

[65] 68th Cong., H. Rept. No. 395, pt. 2.

[66] Cong. Rec., vol. 65, pt. 7, p. 7294.

[67] Ibid., 7288.

Mr. Oliver, of Alabama, moved an amendment that the power conferred in the said resolution should not be greater than that exercised by the legislature of any State prior to April, 1924, with reference to the labor of persons under 18 years of age. This was also rejected.[68] An amendment submitted by Mr. McSwain, of South Carolina, with the proviso that " no law enacted under this article shall affect in any way the labor of any child or children on the farm of the parent or parents," was likewise defeated.[69] Mr. Montague, of Virginia, offered an amendment to recommit the resolution with instructions to report same back with the proviso " but not the labor of such persons in the homes and on the farms where they reside." This motion was rejected.[70]

On the final vote, the resolution passed with a vote of 297 yeas to 69 nays.[71]

In the Senate the resolution was strenuously opposed by a few Senators who saw in it a movement toward establishing, as Senator Wadsworth, of New York, said, " an imperial government at Washington, whose territory will be divided into what might be termed Provinces, instead of what we have known as sovereign States." [72]

Senator Reed, of Missouri, moved to amend the resolution so that it would apply to all persons engaged in occupations other than agricultural and horticultural. This amendment was defeated, 38 yeas to 42 nays.[73] His successive amendments attempting to reduce the age

[68] Cong. Rec., vol. 65, pt. 7, p. 7292.

[69] Ibid., p. 7293.

[70] Ibid., p. 7294.

[71] Ibid., p. 7294.

[72] Ibid., p. 9859.

[73] Ibid., p. 10129.

limit to 14 and then to 16 years were also rejected.[74] Senator Dial, of South Carolina, moved to except those children engaged in outdoor employment, but his amendment was also defeated.[75] Another of Senator Reed's amendments provided that Congress shall have power to regulate the labor of persons under 18 years of age and to prohibit such labor in pursuits involving hazard to health, life, or limb. It was rejected.[76]

Senator Bayard, of Delaware, attempted an amendment providing that ratification should be effected by conventions in the several States, but his motion was lost by a vote of 22 yeas to 58 nays.[77]

On June 3, 1924, the original resolution came to a vote and was passed, 61 yeas to 23 nays.[77] It was signed by the Speaker of the House of Representatives and the President pro tempore of the Senate and submitted to the States for ratification by the Secretary of State.[78]

Among the States the proposed amendment fared illy, for by February 1, 1925, thirteen States had defeated the measure in one or both houses of their legislatures, thus making acceptance, for the time at least, impossible. Since that time other States have moved into the rejecting column, and it seems quite unlikely that 36 States will ever be secured to ratify within the "reasonable time" limit set down by the Supreme Court in the case of Dillon *v.* Gloss.[79] One resolution has already been proposed

[74] Cong. Rec., vol. 65, pt. 7, pp. 10139–10140.

[75] Ibid., p. 10140.

[76] Ibid., p. 10141.

[77] Ibid., p. 10142.

[78] Ibid., p. 10303.

[79] 256 U. S. 368. See sec. 85.

asking that this proposed child labor amendment be repealed.[80]

The practical rejection of the child labor amendment was effected by no means on the ground that child labor should not be regulated, but purely on the ground that this regulation was a police power to be wielded by the States, and that placing such power in the Federal Government was a dangerous tendency toward centralized bureaucracy.[81]

In December, 1925, Senator Johnson, of California, introduced a resolution giving Congress and the several States power to provide for the establishment and enforcement of minimum wages for women and children without stipulating an age limit.[82]

52. Lotteries.

During the early days of the Republic not only were lotteries permitted, but they were legalized and many public enterprises were carried through on funds gained from such gambling. The American Congress itself arranged for a national lottery in 1776. The evil intent of such games of chance, however, in time became evident and one by one the various States prohibited their practice. In 1840 Congress passed an act providing for the suppression of all lotteries in the District of Columbia, and in 1890 Congress passed a law forbidding the use of the mails for the purposes of promoting lotteries or gift enterprises of any kind.[83]

[80] App., No. 1248.

[81] Literary Digest, Feb. 7, 1925.

[82] App., No. 1274.

[83] Spofford, A. R. Article on Lotteries in American Historical Association Report for 1892.

More effectually to stamp out the evil, two amendments were introduced in this latter year designed to place the ban of all lotteries under Federal supervision.[84] The last amendment of this nature was submitted in 1892 by Mr. Robertson, of Louisiana, in which State the pernicious business had gotten a firmer hold through the activities of a certain corporation, the Louisiana State Lottery. This corporation had removed to Honduras, but was still operating in the Southern States.[85]

53. Insurance.

Various attempts have been made to extend the application of the interstate-commerce clause (Art. I, sec. 8, cl. 3) to the business of insurance transacted between citizens in different States. The Supreme Court definitely held, however, in Paul *v.* Virginia,[86] that "issuing a policy of insurance is not a transaction of commerce," and that the contracts of insurance "are not interstate transactions, though the parties may be domiciled in different States." This principle has been reaffirmed in other cases.[87] In the face of these decisions it is obvious that the Federal Government can only acquire the power to govern the business of insurance in the States through a constitutional amendment, and in 1906 Mr. Mahon, of Pennsylvania, proposed such an amendment.[88] An-

[84] App., Nos. 42, 45.

[85] App., No. 60. Spofford, Lotteries.

[86] 8 Wall. 182.

[87] Liverpool & London Fire Ins. Co. *v.* Massachusetts; Berry *v.* Mobile Life Insurance Co.; Federal Case No. 1, 358; N. Y. Life Ins. Co. *v.* Cravens (178 U. S. 401). Putney, A. H., Constitutional Law, pp. 391–392.

[88] App., No. 433.

amendment with the same object in view was again twice presented in 1914, and for the fourth and last time in 1915. One of these was presented by Mr. Peters and the other two by Senator Weeks, both of Massachusetts.[89]

The fact that some foreign countries have undertaken the business of insuring their citizens has led at least one of our legislators to the conviction that the United States should do the same. In 1905 Mr. De Armond, of Missouri, offered an amendment stipulating that "Congress shall have the power to provide for the insurance by the United States of the citizens thereof."[90] He reintroduced this measure twice again—in 1905 and 1907.[91]

Under the war power granted it in Article I, section 8, clause 11, Congress passed an act on October 6, 1917, providing for the insuring of all United States soldiers and sailors, but it is quite improbable that the Government will ever go into the business of insuring its citizens.[92] The opinion appears to be quite general now that Congress has about as much jurisdiction as it can efficiently handle, and that any extensions along this line would intensify a movement altogether too prevalent toward unduly interfering with intrastate business.

54. Treason.

If President Garfield had lived over a year after he was shot, as at one time appeared probable, under American law Charles Guiteau, his assailant could not have been convicted of murder. Neither would the Federal Govern-

[89] App., Nos. 739, 741, 813.
[90] App., No. 428.
[91] App., Nos. 468, 527.
[92] Public No. 90 (H. R. 5723), 65th Cong.

ment have had any but a geographical jurisdiction over him for his crime, as the Constitution is silent as to any attack on Federal officers. When President McKinley was assassinated in 1901 this shortcoming again came to mind, and two amendments were introduced to extend the crime of treason to cover attempts to murder the President or Vice President of the United States.[93] The evident anarchistic intent of Leon Czolgosz and the activities of other anarchists throughout the country at about this time [94] led to the incorporation into the latter of these amendments the further extension of clause 1 of section 3, Article III of the Constitution, designating as treasonable conduct the participation in any "agitation, conspiracy, or organization to subvert all government or being a member of any society, whose avowed purpose it is to destroy and annihilate all civil government."

Four other amendments have been proposed on this subject—one by Mr. Blair, of New Hampshire, defining misprision of treason as "setting up or attempting to set up, or advocate, or instruct, or teach the supremacy or authority of any other, or any foreign potentate or pretended potentate, king, prince, or power within the jurisdiction of any State or of the United States," [95] one by Mr. McKenzie, of Illinois, declaring that it shall be treason to give aid to the enemies of the United States by injuring the military, physical, or financial resources of the United States; [96] and two by Mr. Edmonds, of Pennsylvania, declaring that it shall be treason to "incite or attempt to

[93]App., Nos. 338, 348.

[94]Andrews, Benj. E. History of the United States, Vol. V, pp. 378–379.

[95]App., No. 9.

[96]App., No. 1084.

incite by word or deed the establishment of any new form of government in the United States except by amendment to the Constitution.[97]

LIMITATIONS ON POWERS OF CONGRESS

55. Prohibition of special legislation.

The suspicion entertained by some people that individual Members of Congress are generally always interested in, and quite frequently actively engineering the passage of, legislation beneficial to particular private interests, has fostered the resolve that something should be done to prevent any such diversion of public power.

In this field of reform Mr. Springer, of Illinois, has been the most active in Congress. From 1876 to 1890 he urged upon Congress the adoption of an amendment to the Constitution which would effectually prohibit the passage of special legislation. Within this special legislation he enumerated the granting of pensions, land or prize money, relief to any person, or payment of claims against the United States, except to pay the judgments of courts or commissions. Also, the granting to any corporation of any special or exclusive privileges, subsidy, immunity, or franchise. In short, he wished that Congress should be limited in its legislative power to the "enactment of laws general in their application and effect to all sections and persons within the jurisdiction of this Constitution." He introduced a resolution to this effect on nine different occasions.[98]

In recent times Mr. Russell, of Texas, has taken up this crusade against special legislation, and from 1904 to 1909

---

[97] App., Nos. 1094, 1226.

[98] Ames, pp. 252–253; App., No. 29.

he presented to Congress for four times an amendment declaring that "Congress shall not be permitted to pass any private or special law in any case whatsoever where general laws relating to the subject matter thereof are then in force."[99]

56. Expenditures—appropriation bills.

In the endeavor to curb what was considered the growing extravagance of appropriation bills in the latter part of the nineteenth century, an attempt was made three times by Mr. Turner, of Kentucky and once by Mr. Buchanan, of Virginia, to require the recording of yeas and noes on all bills appropriating more than $10,000. It was assumed that with the Members of Congress being required to take open responsibility for measures on which their yea votes indicated an acquaintance with, they would be more careful to analyze each bill before voting for it.[1] In a further attempt to affix responsibility for all expenditures, the last of these measures included the provision that no money bill should become law unless it had the affirmative vote of a majority of all Members elected to each House.

The practice of linking up an unpopular measure with a bill of importance in order to insure the passage of the former, has led to the consideration of a constitutional amendment designed to prevent the incorporation of more than one subject in bills before Congress. Such an amendment has now been proposed three times, the first two requiring that every act shall contain but one subject matter, and the matter properly connected therewith,

[99] App., Nos. 402, 454, 461, 547.

[1] Ames, p. 251; App. No. 87.

which shall be declared in the title, and the last one providing for the same prohibition except in appropriation bills.[2]

57. Claims against the United States.

On February 24, 1855, Congress established what is known as the Court of Claims. This court has jurisdiction of all "claims founded upon the Constitution of the United States or any law of Congress, except for pensions, or upon any regulations of an executive department, or upon any contract, express or implied, with the Government of the United States, or for damages, liquidated or unliquidated, in cases not sounding in tort, in respect of which claims the party would be entitled to redress against the United States, either in a court of law, equity, or admiralty, if the United States were suable, except claims growing out of the late Civil War and commonly known as war claims."[3]

It has been assumed by some that the jurisdiction of this court has not been extensive enough, and that it still leaves to Congress a wide political jurisdiction over matters that are in nature judicial questions. As Congress, however, has the exclusive power to appropriate money from the United States Treasury, it has been impossible to confer upon any tribunal a right or privilege which would in any way conflict with this exclusive grant of appropriating jurisdiction. Three attempts have, therefore, been made to amend the Constitution so as to curtail the powers of Congress with regard to the appropriation of public moneys by conferring a larger jurisdiction

[2] Ames, p. 251; App., No. 961.

[3] Cong. Direct., 67th Cong., 2d sess., p. 381, citing 10 Stat. L., 612.

on a Court of Claims.[4] All these resolutions were introduced by Mr. Keifer, of Ohio, and the last one presented in 1909 declares that "Congress shall have no power to appropriate money for the payment of any claim against the United States unless preferred by a State thereof, not created in pursuance of, or previously authorized by, law, international treaty, or award, except in payment of a final judgment rendered thereon by a court or tribunal having competent jurisdiction." It also provided for the establishment of such a competent court of claims.[5]

58. Chartering corporations.

The fear entertained by many of the colonists that the new Federal Government might duplicate the errors of foreign governments in granting commercial monopolies such as the British East India Company and the Dutch East India Company prompted five of the State ratifying conventions to propose an amendment declaring that Congress shall erect "no company of merchants with exclusive advantage of commerce."[6] The fact that this proposed amendment was not accepted was probably due to the conviction maintained by many that since the Federal Government was but one of delegated powers, all powers of incorporation remained in the States. This contention was brought forth in the famous case of McCulloch *v.* Maryland.[7] The decision in that case led to the presentation by the Legislatures of Pennsylvania,

[4] App., Nos. 426, 472, 550.

[5] App., No. 550.

[6] Ames, p. 255.

[7] Beveridge, Albert J. Life of John Marshall, vol. 3, ch. 3, pp. 101–156.

Tennessee, Ohio, Indiana, and Illinois of a proposal to restrict Congress to the District of Columbia in the establishment of any bank. The fear of these States as to the possible encroachment of Congress upon State incorporating powers was not shared by the other States and no amendment resulted. In 1833, however, the Legislature of Georgia recommended that the constitutional convention, which it requested be convened, should discuss the question as to whether the power of chartering a bank and of granting incorporation should be "expressly given to or withheld from Congress." No action was taken in this matter, and the last proposal, indicating a desire to circumscribe the incorporating powers of Congress, was advanced in 1872, declaring that Congress should hereafter be prohibited from chartering private corporations to carry on business within the State.[8]

In recent years there has been a general dissipation of the fear that Congress might unduly interfere with the interior business of the respective States, and, on the contrary, there has been a movement toward a centralized control of all corporations. Mr. McDermott, of New Jersey, has been an active protagonist of the theory that Congress should be the mother power to create the corporations of the entire country. From 1900 to 1904 he introduced four times in Congress a resolution providing that the Constitution should be so amended as to give Congress power to "pass general laws under which corporations may be organized and corporate powers of every nature obtained and controlled." Also that laws should be passed governing the activities of foreign corporations, and that the States should be permitted to

[8]Ames, p. 257.

charter only corporations engaged in banking and insurance.[9]

An amendment pertaining to corporations, but of a much milder nature than that proposed by Mr. McDermott, was that introduced by Mr. Crumpacker, of Indiana, in 1901 providing that " Congress shall have power to tax the capital stock and earnings of all private corporations carried on for purposes of gain, without regard to the population of the States, and such tax may be progressive.[10]

TERRITORIAL POWERS

59. Admission of Territories into the United States.

Although the subject of Territories has been a prolific source of discussion in the documents of Congress and Supreme Court Reports, it is interesting to observe the rarity of proposed amendments on the subject. This is additionally interesting when we remember that the Constitution says nothing about the annexation of territory, and is very vague as to the government and regulation of it. (Art. IV, sec. 3.)

With the exception of the pre-Civil War amendments proposed to regulate the establishment of slavery in the Territories no formal attempts have been made to add to the Constitution any article regarding the disposition of Territories.[11] A number of amendments have been introduced, however, governing the admission of new States made up from Territories. The first one in this respect was presented in 1815 and stipulated that a two-thirds

[9]App., Nos. 315, 323, 356, 405.
[10]App., No. 346.
[11]Ames, p. 176.

concurring vote of both Houses of Congress was necessary to admit a new State. In 1871 another amendment was introduced declaring that no Territory or District should be considered for admission as a State unless it had at least enough population to entitle it to one Representative in Congress according to the ratio of representation at that time.[12]

Commencing with 1896 a series of amendments were submitted covering this subject. The first one, presented by Mr. Fenton, of Ohio, on March 5, 1896, provided that " No addition shall ever be made to the number of States constituting the Union from any Territory which may hereafter be acquired by the United States if such Territory lie south of the parallel of 30° north latitude. But in the event of the acquisition by the United States of any Territory thus situated the Congress shall forever exercise exclusive legislation in all cases whatsoever over such Territory." [13] This amendment was undoubtedly proposed to keep Hawaii out of the Union, the most northern point of Hawaii being 22° 15′ north latitude. The treaty, which had been withdrawn from the consideration of the Senate by President Cleveland in 1893, provided that the Hawaiian Islands should become an integral part of the United States, and it was expected that at any time the treaty would be returned to the Senate.[14]

The second one of this series was championed by Mr. Crumpacker, of Indiana, and it declared that no noncontiguous territory should ever become part of the United States except by a treaty negotiated by the President and ratified by two-thirds of both Houses of Congress and

[12]Ames, p. 180.

[13]App., No. 188.

[14] Latane, America as a World Power, pp. 136–137.

three-fourths of the State legislatures.[15] This amendment, introduced June 28, 1897, was also prompted by the Hawaiian question, and was designed to thwart the plans of the expansionists who, realizing the impossibility of getting favorable action in the Senate on the treaty of June, 1897, presented by President McKinley, were contemplating the achieving of their object by a joint resolution.[16]

Mr. Crumpacker's resolution also included a section providing that contiguous territory should be admitted only after a treaty and two-thirds favorable vote of both Houses, the House voting two years after the Senate.

Two amendments of a more restrictive nature were proposed by Mr. Cooney, of Missouri, one in 1897 and the other in 1900. They declared categorically that non-contiguous territory should never be admitted to the Union.[17]

By joint resolution signed July 7, 1898, the United States acquired the Hawaiian Islands.[18] On February 6, 1899, the treaty with Spain was ratified by the Senate, and the Philippines, Porto Rico, and Guam came under American dominion.[19] As many Members of Congress had opposed the annexation of this territory, it was assumed that there would be as many, if not more, opposed to the idea of admitting any part of it into the Union as a State or States. Accordingly, the amendment introduced by Mr. Hepburn, of Iowa, stipulating that territory acquired after January 1, 1898, should be admitted to the

[15] App., No. 226.
[16] Latane, America as a World Power, p. 138.
[17] App., Nos. 233, 299.
[18] Latane, America as a World Power, p. 139.
[19] Ibid., p. 77.

Union only after a three-fourths affirmative vote of all Members elected to both Houses of Congress, was calculated to effectually delay, if not wholly prevent, the incorporation of any of this territory into the Union.[20]

The last two amendments of this series were designed entirely to prohibit these annexations from becoming States. One was presented by Mr. Gillett, of Massachusetts, on April 11, 1900, and declared that no territory acquired after January 1, 1895, could be admitted to the Union, and the other introduced on April 19, 1902, by Mr. Wadsworth, of New York, provided that "hereafter no territory not embraced within the geographical limits of continental North America shall be admitted as a State."[21]

An amendment submitted by Mr. Towner, of Iowa, in 1921 declared that Congress shall determine the representation in Congress of all United States Territories with the limitation that the senatorial and congressional representation shall not exceed that permitted the States of the Union.[22]

60. The District of Columbia.

The admission of all Territories in continental United States into the Union has left the District of Columbia the only continental geographical division without statehood. This anomalous situation is heightened by the fact that since 1874 the citizens of this District have not had the right of suffrage. They acordingly take no part in the selection of the administration officers, which consist of three commissioners chosen by the President with the

[20]App., No. 249.
[21]App., Nos. 311, 369.
[22]App., No. 1059.

concurrence of the Senate. They also have no representative in the House of Representatives or the Senate.[23]

This has been considered by some Members of Congress quite an irregularity in American democracy, and numerous attempts have been made to remedy the declared defect by constitutional amendment. The first amendment of this nature was introduced in 1888 by Senator Blair, of New Hampshire, and provided for District representation in the two Houses of Congress and votes in the Electoral College.[24] In 1889 he introduced two other measures, the first declaring for a representation of one Senator and as many Representatives as the population called for according to the ratio in effect on that date, and the second calling for the same representation with the proviso that "such representation shall not participate in the joint convention of the two Houses, nor in any proceeding touching the choice of President and Vice President, nor any organization of either House of Congress, nor speak or vote upon any question concerning same."[25] Both of these amendments were reported back to the Senate by the Committee on Privileges and Elections with the recommendation that they do not pass,[26] and after a little consideration were passed over without vote.

In 1902, Senator Gallinger, also of New Hampshire, renewed the request for District representation. His amendment stipulated that the District of Columbia should be considered a State for the purposes of congressional representation and vote in the Electoral College.[27]

[23] Bryan, W. B. Forms of Local Government in District of Columbia, pp. 24–26.

[24] Ames, p. 181.

[25] App., Nos. 6, 8.

[26] Cong. Rec., 51st Cong., 1st sess., pp. 297, 802.

[27] App., No. 374.

Nothing further was done to give the District representation by way of constitutional amendment until 1915, when a series of resolutions with this object in view was started. From 1915 to 1919, 10 amendments of this nature were introduced; 7 of these declared for straight State representation;[28] 1 provided for the single Senator and as many Representatives as the population called for;[29] and 2 merely indicated that suffrage should be given to the citizens of the District of Columbia.[30] In order that there might be no doubt as to the rights of the citizens of the District of Columbia in the courts of the United States, this question having once been agitated,[31] two of the amendments above enumerated contained the additional provision that citizens of the District should be considered as citizens of a State for the purpose of suing and being sued in the courts of the United States.[32]

During the Sixty-seventh, Sixty-eighth, Sixty-ninth, and Seventieth Congresses eight resolutions were introduced providing that Congress shall have power to admit to the status of State citizens the residents of the District of Columbia; that the District of Columbia shall be entitled to one or two Senators as Congress may determine and as many Representatives as the census figures provide for, and that Congress shall indicate by law the qualifications of voters and the time and manner of choosing Senators and Representatives.[33]

[28] App, Nos. 793, 805, 863, 889, 916, 917, 1001.

[29] App., No. 943.

[30] App., No. 982.

[31] Bacon, American Plan of Government, p. 399, citing Callan *v.* Wilson (127 U. S. Rep. 540).

[32] App., Nos. 863, 943.

[33] App., Nos. 1036, 1087, 1179, 1199, 1270, 1291, 1312, 1327.

One of these resolutions (S. J. Res. 133, 67th Cong.) was acted upon favorably by the Senate Committee on the District of Columbia (67th Cong.) and reported back to the Senate with a recommendation that it be passed. The report accompanying the resolution pointed out that under the power to admit new States and to regulate territory belonging to the United States, Congress now has the authority to admit to representation in Congress and the Electoral College the people of all the territory belonging to the United States except the district constituting the seat of government of the United States. The constitutional provision giving Congress the power of exclusive legislation in the seat of government deprives Congress of the power to admit the seat of government to congressional representation through the gate of statehood, since full statehood for the District would destroy the exclusive power of legislation in the District bestowed upon Congress by the Constitution. Accordingly, the only way to give to the people of the District of Columbia representation, with access to the Federal courts, is by an amendment to the Constitution.

Arguing that the people of the District should receive some of the privileges of statehood it was demonstrated that the census for 1920 shows that the District of Columbia has a population greater than that of any one of the seven States of Nevada, Wyoming, Delaware, Arizona, Vermont, New Mexico, and Idaho. Further, that the records for the fiscal year ending June 30, 1919, disclose that the citizens of the District of Columbia paid to the Government taxes in the sum of $18,645,053, which amount was greater than the aggregate of similar taxes paid by the States of South Dakota, New Mexico, Nevada, Wyoming, and Vermont combined.[34]

The Committee on the District of Columbia, in deliberating on Senate Joint Resolution No. 7, Sixty-ninth Congress, adopted as its own this same report made on Senate Joint Resolution No. 133, Sixty-seventh Congress, and just here discussed.[35]

Of the many resolutions providing for District of Columbia representation introduced in Congress, none has yet come to a direct vote.

FEDERAL TAXATION

61. Direct taxes.

The prohibition in the Constitution regarding the levying of direct taxes except according to population was aimed to protect the thinly populated States. It would be manifestly unfair to levy the same tax on real estate in South Carolina, with its large extent of territory but comparatively few people, as would be levied for instance in Massachusetts with its small territory but large population.[36]

Some question early arose as to the meaning of " direct taxes " as used in the Constitution, and in an effort to make this clear an amendment was introduced in 1793 providing that every tax should be deemed direct, other than taxes on imports, excises, transfers of property, and law proceedings.[37] In interpreting a law passed by Con-

[34] 67th Cong., 2d sess. S. Rept. No. 507.

[35] 69th Cong., S. Rept. No. 1515.

[36] Bacon, American Plan of Government, p. 57.

[37] Ames, p. 243.

gress in 1794 taxing carriages, the Supreme Court held that such a tax was not direct in the meaning of the Constitution, but that such "direct" taxes referred only to poll tax or tax on land.[38]

During the first century of constitutional history 18 other amendments were introduced touching this subject, but they all referred to the manner of the apportionment of direct taxes. Some of these provided that direct taxes should be apportioned among the several States according to the number of their free inhabitants, some according to the appraised value of taxable property therein, and others according to the numbers of United States citizens in the respective States.[39] The last two amendments on this point were presented by Mr. Crain, of Texas, in 1893, and by Mr. Kitchin, of North Carolina, in 1902. They both declared that direct taxes should be apportioned according to the assessed valuation of all property subject to taxation under the laws of the several States.[40]

The last direct tax was imposed in 1861 and was refunded to the States by the Federal Government in 1891.[41] It was therefore apparent that the central Government had about abandoned the idea of a purely direct tax, probably assuring itself that an income tax could always be counted upon in financial exigencies. Although for a hundred years it was generally believed that income taxes did not fall within the prohibition of "direct taxes," the decision of the Supreme Court in 1895 in the Pollock case[42] overturned this conviction and prompted many legislators

[38] 3 Dallas Rep. 171.

[39] Ames, pp. 244, 245.

[40] App., Nos. 138, 368.

[41] Dewey, D. R. National Problems, p. 186.

[42] 157 U. S. Rep. 430.

to propose the entire abolition of the ban on direct taxes. One of these preceded the Supreme Court's decision and was introduced in 1893 by Mr. McRae, of Arkansas, and was therefore probably based on some other reason.[43] In the years 1895, 1898, 1907, and 1912 four amendments were presented which proposed to authorize Congress to levy direct taxes without limitation.[44]

The bulk of the amendments touching the subject of taxation which came after the Pollock decision stated merely that Congress should have power to levy an income tax, and this subject is discussed in the section on the sixteenth amendment.[45]

A resolution introduced in 1921 and two more in 1925 declared that the enumeration necessary in order to apportion uniformly the direct taxes provided for in clause 3, section 2, Article I, of the Constitution shall be made every 10 years in such manner as Congress shall by law direct.[46]

In 1922, Mr. Layton, of Delaware, introduced an amendment designed to prohibit Congress from laying and collecting any income taxes except to defray the expenses of actual war.[47]

62. Inheritance taxes.

The Federal Government has several times imposed inheritance taxes, and the constitutionality of the inheritance-tax provisions of the Federal law was directly upheld in the case of Knowlton *v.* Moore.[48] Numerous

[43] App., No. 136.
[44] App., Nos. 154, 247, 475, 654.
[45] Sec. No. 88.
[46] App., Nos. 1051, 1066, 1254.
[47] App., No. 1109.
[48] Willoughby, Constitutional Law, p. 218, citing 178 U. S. 41.

amendments nevertheless have been presented specifically giving Congress this power and thus avoid the possibility of any reversing decision like that in the Pollock case. Ten amendments, therefore, some treating this subject exclusively and others incorporating other tax provisions, have declared for authorizing Congress to levy inheritance taxes.[49] Two of this number have declared the minimum estate subject to such taxation to be $50,000 and one $100,000.[50]

63. Taxation of State securities, Federal and State officers, and stock dividends.

On December 28, 1920, Mr. McFadden, of Pennsylvania, offered an amendment declaring that "Congress can collect taxes on income derived from securities created by the States and their subsidiary governments," and "salaries of all public officials, Federal as well as State, elected or appointed to office after the ratification of this article, without apportionment among the States and without regard to any census or enumeration."[51] The Pollock case had decided that that part of the law of 1894 levying taxes upon the income derived from municipal bonds interfered with the power of the States and their instrumentalities to borrow money and was therefore void as being repugnant to the Constitution.[52]

So as not to conflict with the provisions of the Constitution (Art. II, sec. 1, cl. 6, and Art. III, sec. 1) declaring, respectively, that the compensation of the President and Federal judges shall not be decreased during term of

[49] App., Nos. 180, 230, 457, 458, 490, 535, 536, 749, 1018, 1233.

[50] App., Nos. 457, 490, 180.

[51] App., No. 1030.

[52] 157 U. S., 429.

office, Congress exempted in the income tax law of 1916, the "compensation of the present President of the United States during the term for which he has been elected, and the judges of the Supreme and inferior courts of the United States now in office.[53] The latter part of Mr. McFadden's amendment was designed to make such exemptions unnecessary.

On March 8, 1920, the Supreme Court decided in Eisner *v.* Macomber[54] that stock dividends which were made against the accumulated profits of a corporation since the adoption of the sixteenth amendment could not be considered as income, and that the constitutional prohibition against the taxation by Congress without apportionment of a stockholder's interest in the undivided accumulated earnings of a corporation is not removed by the adoption of the income-tax amendment. This decision was rendered by a divided court and was severely criticized throughout the country. About two weeks later Senator Nelson, of Minnesota, proposed an amendment to the Constitution designed to counteract the effect of the Supreme Court's decision by authorizing Congress to collect taxes on all incomes, including stock dividends.[55]

RECIPROCAL TAXATION

On December 8, 1925, and again on December 5, 1927, Mr. Garber, of Oklahoma, introduced a resolution to the effect that the United States shall have power to levy and collect taxes on income derived from securities issued by or under the authority of any State, but without dis-

[53] App., No. 1030.
[54] 39 Stat. 758 (6336d, ch. 43, 4).
[55] App., No. 1018.

crimination against income derived from such securities and in favor of income derived from securities issued after the ratification of this article by or under the authority of the United States or any State. Further, that each State shall have similar power but without discrimination against income derived from such securities and in favor of income derived from securities issued by or under the authority of such State.[56] On February 3, 1928, Mr. Hogg, of Indiana, introduced an identical constitutional amendment.[57]

On December 8, 1925, Mr. Oliver, of New York, introduced a similar resolution with the additional provision that Congress shall provide that moneys so collected by the United States or any State shall be returned to the Federal or State Government that issued said securities.[58] He reintroduced this resolution on December 5, 1927.[59]

CONSTITUTIONAL AMENDMENTS ON SUBJECT OF TAX-EXEMPT SECURITIES

In his message to Congress on December 6, 1921, President Harding said:

> I think our tax problems, the tendency of wealth to seek nontaxable investment, and the menacing increase of public debt, Federal, State, and municipal, all justify a proposal to change the Constitution so as to end the issue of nontaxable bonds.[60]

This declaration marks the beginning of a series of resolutions designed to amend the Constitution on the subject of tax-exempt securities. So far 11 have been

[56] App., No. 1276, 1316.
[57] App., No. 1347.
[58] App., No. 1282.
[59] App., No 1321.
[60] H. Rept. No. 30, 68th Cong., p. 4.

submitted providing that Congress shall have power to tax income derived from securities issued by the United States or any other State.[61] Nine of these amendments provide that the States may tax securities of the United States but without discrimination against such securities in favor of its own. Five other amendments declare merely that Congress shall have the power to tax securities held by the individual States.[62]

The arguments in favor of an abolition of tax-exempt securities center around the fact that there are at present from what has been variously estimated, from $10,000,000,000 to $18,000,000,000 of such preferred securities. It was the opinion of the House Committee on Ways and Means of the 67th and 68th Congresses[63] that such a situation should be condemned for eight reasons:

1. A large portion of property escapes taxation, thereby causing great loss of revenue.
2. It violates the ability principle of taxation and unfairly discriminates between taxpayers.
3. It impedes private financing.
4. It discourages investment in new enterprises.
5. It encourages extravagances of governmental agencies.
6. It grants a private subsidy to certain interests.
7. By withdrawing money from private enterprises it increases the rate of interest required for all enterprises not carried on by the Government and thereby adds to the cost of living.
8. It creates social unrest.

It was estimated that in 1921 over a billion dollars was issued of tax-exempt securities and that the "amount in existence is constantly increasing."[64]

---

[61] App., Nos. 1065, 1085, 1100, 1127, 1147, 1212, 1229, 1230, 1233, 1236, 1253.

[62] App., Nos. 1082, 1089, 1090, 1186, 1240.

[63] 67th Cong., H. Rept. No. 969; 68th Cong., H. Rept. No. 30.

[64] Ibid.

Secretary of Treasury Mellon writing to the Committee on Ways and Means on April 30, 1921, on the subject, declared " every increasing volume of tax-exempt securities (issued for the most part by State and municipalities) represents a grave economic evil, not only by reason of loss of revenue which it entails to the Federal Government, but also because of its tendency to increase the growth of public indebtedness and to direct capital to productive enterprises. The issue of tax-exempt securities has the direct tendency to make the graduated Federal surtax ineffective and nonproductive because it enables taxpayers subject to surtaxes to reduce the amount of their taxable income by investing it in such securities, and at the same time the result is that a very large class of capital investments escape their just share of taxation." [65]

In opposition it has been declared that a constitutional amendment of this nature would be an " invasion of the fundamental distinction founded by the fathers of the Republic when the Government was created." It would " rob each State of one element of its sovereignty." Also, while the resolutions propose an element of reciprocity between the Federal Government and the State governments, in actuality the State " loses infinitely more than the Government of the United States gains." [66]

It was claimed further that the credit of every State would be impaired by such an amendment; and that they would be unable to realize on their bond issues. "A necessity will arise in a community that is not blessed with a great credit like the United States and it will wish

[65] 67th Cong., H. Rept. No. 969; 68th Cong., H. Rept. No. 30.

[66] Speech of Mr. Graham, of Pennsylvania, Dec. 19, 1922. Cong. Rec., vol. 64, pt. 1, p. 726.

to raise money by bonds for the purpose of some little necessary improvement in its midst, and if faced by this possible double taxation of income, the State will be powerless to carry out its purpose." [67]

The resolutions adopted by the United States Good Roads Association in convention at Greensburg, S. C., on April 16 and 17, 1923, fairly epitomize the objections to the amendment:

1. The proposed constitutional amendment would give the United States Government power to tax the income from all future issues of Federal, State, local, and municipal bonds. The States would be given a similar privilege with respect to future Federal bonds held by residents within their borders.

2. The power of the Federal Government to tax the instruments of the States would give the power to regulate or control their activities. This is a flagrant violation of the principle of State rights.

3. The proposed measure is neither necessary nor expedient. The total amount of tax-exempt bonds outstanding has been grossly exaggerated, and at least one-half of the total outstanding is held by institutions and funds that can not be reached by law since they are tax exempt by State charters. Since probably one-half the remainder of all tax-exempt bonds are held by small investors, to whom the exemption is slight, not more than a quarter of the total could possibly be held by wealthy tax dodgers. As soon as the maximum surtax rate is reduced below 25 to 30 per cent, as will probably be done in another year or two, the opportunity for this kind of tax dodging will rapidly vanish.

4. The proposed measure would seriously curtail public improvements, particularly road building. The interest rate on bonds would be raised at least 1 per cent. This would mean an even added burden to the local taxpayer and proportionately greater difficulty in getting popular authorization for new bond issues, and increased difficulty in selling the bonds might be encountered because of tax-rate uncertainties.[68]

[67] Speech of Mr. Graham, of Pennsylvania, Dec. 19, 1922. Cong. Rec., vol. 64, pt. 1, p. 727.

[68] Cong. Rec., vol. 64, pt. 1, p. 2016.

Mr. Bankhead, of Alabama, pointed out, in opposition also, that such an amendment would be " almost destructive of our Federal farm-loan banking system which has been of such tremendous importance to the farmer everywhere, especially in the South and West. Before the adoption of that system the average interest charged against farmers for short-term loans was from 8 to 15 per cent. The average rate to them now is about 6 per cent. The tax-exempt feature of the bonds of the system is entirely and solely responsible for the low rate of interest now prevailing. It is conceded that if the exemption be removed the interest rate would at once increase from 1 to 2 per cent." [69]

The resolution proposed by Mr. Green, of Iowa, on April 28, 1922, came on for a vote in the House of Representatives on January 23, 1923, and was approved, 223 yeas to 101 nays.[70] Attempts to amend the resolution to exclude all except those who owned Federal and State securities exceeding $100,000; to have the amendment passed on by State conventions rather than State legislatures; to exclude all securities issued under the provisions of the Federal farm loan act; to provide for a 5-year limit for ratification, were all rejected.[71] On January 24, 1923, the approved resolution was referred to the Senate Committee on the Judiciary, from which it did not emerge.

Upon the commencement of the Sixty-eighth Congress Mr. Green reintroduced his resolution and succeeded in bringing it again before the House. This time, however, it failed, the vote being 247 yeas to 133 nays, or less than two-thirds, the majority required by the Constitution.[72]

---

[69] Cong. Rec., vol. 65, pt. 2, pp. 2013, 2014.

[70] Cong. Rec., vol. 64, pt. 1, p. 2383.

[71] Ibid., pp. 2278–2283.

[72] Cong. Rec., vol. 65, pt. 3, p. 2142, Feb. 8, 1924.

64. Taxation of corporations by States.

Five attempts have been made to remove the restriction in Article I, section 10, clause 3, of the Constitution forbidding any State to pass a law impairing the obligations of contracts.[73] The State of Maryland was responsible for these proposals, which were presented in Congress from 1884 to 1889 by Mr. McComas, of that State. The last one provided that "no State shall be precluded by the grant of any charter or act of incorporation from taxing the capital stock or property of such corporation; nor shall any charter or act of incorporation heretofore granted or that may hereafter be granted by any State be construed to preclude the State from the power of taxation; but the States shall have and retain the full power and right of taxation as if the prohibition to pass laws impairing the obligation of contracts had never been incorporated in this Constitution."

This proposal was prompted by the great increase in the number, wealth, and power of corporations since the decision in the Dartmouth College case.[74]

65. Uniformity of taxation and capitation tax.

On December 21, 1895, Mr. Hall, of Missouri, introduced a resolution designed to bring about uniformity in taxes, as well as in "duties, imposts, and excises," as required by Article I, section 8, clause 1, of the Constitution. There was added to this amendment the proviso that "all capitation taxes shall, and any other tax may, be apportioned among the several States according to their respective number, counting the whole number of persons

[73]Ames, pp. 245–246; App., No. 22.

[74]Ames, pp. 245–246.

in each State, excluding Indians not taxed." [75] A similar amendment was presented by Mr. McRae, of Arkansas, in 1897.[76]

An amendment proposed by Mr. Sanford, of North Carolina to authorize Congress to collect an income tax included the provision that it must be uniform throughout the United States.[77] Such a provision is quite unnecessary, for with the definition that a "tax is uniform when it operates with the same force and effect in every place where the subject of it is found," [78] it is hardly to be expected that Congress would discriminate against, or in favor of, any particular State.

66. The initiative, referendum, and recall.

The last quarter of the nineteenth century saw strictly representative government and democratic government contesting for supremacy in the country. The uncovering of many alleged abuses of the representative system started a movement for a more direct popular control over government.[79] In the presidential campaign of 1896 the attacks of Colonel Bryan, as leader of the Democratic Party, on so-called plutocratic government, merged with a nation-wide movement for political reform.[80] These activities brought about the establishment in various States of senatorial and presidential primaries, woman suffrage, and other measures calculated to bring about the

[75] App., No. 175.

[76] App., No. 214.

[77] App., No. 234.

[78] Head Money Cases, 112 U. S. Rep. 581.

[79] Oberholtzer. The Referendum in America. Chapter XIX, The Referendum *v.* The Representative System, pp. 471–513.

[80] Ogg. National Progress, p. 147.

instrumentalities of government under the direct control of the people.[81] The most revolutionary and far-reaching of these measures were the initiative, referendum, and recall.[82]

67. The initiative and referendum.

Although the referendum was a well-known institution in the early part of the nineteenth century and by 1850 was used almost universally in the adoption of State constitutions and amendments, its twin-brother, the initiative, did not gain any recognition until the last decade of that century. In 1898 the referendum and initiative for ordinary legislation was adopted by the State of South Dakota; [83] in 1900 Utah took the same step,[84] and by 1917 the system was being used in 18 States.[85]

This trend throughout the country toward a greater democratization of government was naturally reflected in the Federal legislature, and brought about the introduction between 1907 and 1921 of over a score of amendments designed in some form or another to establish the initiative and referendum in the Federal Government.

The pioneer amendment in this field antedated even the State laws, and was introduced in 1895 by Senator Peffer, of Kansas. It stipulated that "On petition of one-fifth of the qualified electors of the United States, or on request of one-fifth of the legislatures of the States, Congress shall

[81] Ogg. National Progress, Chapter IX, Democracy and Responsibility in Government, pp. 147–161.

[82] Oberholtzer. See Chapter XVI, The Initiative and Referendum in the State, pp. 391–426.

[83] Ibid., p. 385.

[84] Ibid., p. 396.

[85] Ogg. National Progress, pp. 161–162.

submit to a vote of the people any matter presented in such petition or request." Further, that "No law to change or alter the established policy of the United States in any great matter of administration and especially respecting our foreign relations, the public lands, taxation, and our monetary system shall take effect until it has been approved by the people at an election held for that purpose."[86]

In 1911 Mr. Fulton, of Oklahoma, presented an amendment designating that 8 per cent of the voters of not less than 15 States and 10 per cent of the same number of voters could, respectively, propose bills and constitutional amendments, and that 5 per cent of the voters of 15 States could demand a referendum.[87] In this same year an amendment of an extreme and radical nature was introduced by Mr. Berger, of Wisconsin. It declared that the House of Representatives should have exclusive power of legislation, be responsible to no institution (President or Supreme Court, the Senate to be abolished) except the people who could by a petition of 5 per cent of the qualified voters for members of the lower houses of the State legislatures in each of three-fourths of the States, demand a referendum, within 90 days after passage, of any law of the House of Representatives, and that upon such referendum a majority of all the votes cast should declare its effectiveness or nullity.[88]

Two amendments introduced in 1919 declared for the submission to the people for acceptance or rejection of any law or constitutional amendment proposed, respec-

[86]App., No. 164.
[87]App., No. 478.
[88]App., No. 608.

tively, by 500,000 or 1,000,000 bona fide voters of the United States.[89]

A resolution presented in 1921 by Mr. Morin, of Pennsylvania, and one by Mr. Dyer, of Missouri, in 1928, provided that upon presentation of a petition signed by 500,000 voters, the Secretary of State would be required to submit the question involved to the people at the next congressional election; and if signed by 1,000,000 at a special election to be called.[90]

A referendum amendment of an unusual nature under our system of government with the legislative and executive departments quite distinctly set apart, was that presented by Senator Bristow, of Kansas, declaring that if Congress fails to enact measures recommended by the President he shall refer such measures to the people for determination at the next regular congressional election.[91]

The extremest of the initiative amendments was that submitted by Mr. Miller, of Wisconsin, declaring that one one-thousandth of the people who are to be affected by a proposed law may ask for its submission to the people for ratification.[92]

The three amendments referring to a referendum on laws declared unconstitutional by the Supreme Court,[93] and the 12 amendments designed to bring about the initiation and ratification of proposed constitutional amend-

[89]App., Nos. 996, 994.
[90]App., No. 1067, 1350.
[91]App., No. 658.
[92]App., No. 114.
[93]App., Nos. 653, 659, 676.

ments by direct vote of the people [94] are discussed elsewhere in this monograph.[95] The referendum amendment declaring that the people shall vote on all treaties affecting the sovereignty and territory of the United States is also listed in another section.[96]

68. The recall.

Another institution of direct popular government, the adoption of which has been much agitated during recent years, is the recall. It was first used in the city of Los Angeles in 1903, and the first State to adopt it was Oregon, in 1908. By 1914, 10 States had recall provisions in their constitutions.[97]

The initial amendment on this subject in Congress was presented by Mr. Fulton, of Oklahoma in 1907 and provided that 33⅓ per cent of the voters of a congressional district could demand a vote on the recall of their representative, and if it failed 75 per cent was necessary to call a second vote.[98] Four other amendments, providing for increasing the term of Representatives (two to four years and two to six years) included also the provision for recalls.[99]

The recall was not very favorably received in Congress, especially in its application to judges. When in 1912 President Taft vetoed the resolution accepting the Arizona constitution because that constitution contained

[94] App., Nos. 705, 708, 717, 763, 778, 806, 851, 859, 926, 933, 966, 1019.

[95] Chapters III, V.

[96] App., No. 1031; sec. 44.

[97] Munro, Wm. B. Initiative, Referendum, and Recall, p. 43.

[98] App., No. 477.

[99] Sec. 5.

the judicial recall, Congress immediately passed another resolution providing that Arizona would be admitted to the Union only on condition that the recall of judges be wholly stricken from its constitution.[1]

In a speech on the subject of judicial recall, Senator Crawford, of South Dakota, said that this "sword of Damocles should not hang over a judge. The tenure of office held by him should never be made to depend upon the decision of the majority of the voters in his district, expressed by ballot at the close of a heated campaign, forced upon him by a minority petition signed ex parte; a campaign in which the issue is whether or not he correctly weighed the testimony and applied the law in the causes tried by him."[2]

Only three amendments have been presented in Congress on the subject of judicial recall, and one of these referred to cases where the judge in question has commited "treason, bribery, or other high crime or misdemeanor."[3]

THE QUESTION OF ALIENS

69. Right to vote at Federal elections.

The right to vote at a Federal election springs from the Constitution of the United States and therefore is a Federal guarantee (that is, there are specific provisions in the Constitution which state that Representatives and Senators shall be elected by those having the right in each State to vote for the members of the most numerous branch of the State legislature, Art. I, sec. 2; Amend-

[1] Ogg, National Progress, p. 165.
[2] Cong. Rec., May 23, 1912, p. 6399.
[3] App., Nos. 628, 649, 688.

ment XVII), but the right of determining the conditions upon which the suffrage may be granted (excepting the fifteenth amendment) lies exclusively within the discretion of the several States.[4] It is therefore possible for a Federal citizen to be denied the vote, and for a person not a Federal citizen to be given the suffrage. Under this latter condition many persons throughout the country participate in Federal elections before they have been naturalized and declared citizens of the United States.[5]

In an effort to stop this practice, and at the same time offer an incentive to aliens toward acquiring Federal citizenship, measures have been recommended leading to the disfranchisement of all aliens. Eleven amendments have already been offered stipulating that no State shall grant the suffrage to any one not a citizen of the United States.[6]

The first amendment touching this subject was introduced by Mr. Langston, of Virginia, in 1890, and declared that the Federal suffrage should be limited to those who can read and write English. Further, that representation in the House of Representatives should be reduced proportionate to such illiterate population.[7] Another resolution requiring the literacy test was introduced in 1895. This amendment declared that no alien should be per-

[4] Willoughby, Constitutional Law of U. S., p. 190.

[5] Munro, Wm. B. Government of American Cities, p. 107. The States of Alabama, Arkansas, Kansas, Indiana, Missouri, Nebraska, Oregon, South Dakota, and Texas all allow noncitizens to vote.

[6] App., Nos. 54, 158, 160, 178, 242, 940, 948, 951, 952, 959; No. 178 also provides that no alien shall hold any Federal or State office.

[7] App., No. 48. The second provision of this amendment may have been intended as a means of retaliation against the Northern States for their threat to enforce reduction of southern representation based upon the denial of the vote to negroes, as provided for in the fourteenth amendment.

mitted to vote until he had resided in this country at least five years, and was a citizen of the United States at least six months and a citizen of the State or Territory at least one year prior to the election. Also that he must be able to read and write the Constitution.[8]

Although the Constitution declares that the electors of Representatives and Senators shall have the qualifications requisite for electors of the most numerous branch of the State legislatures, it does not place the same restriction upon those voting for the electors of the President and Vice President. Accordingly, Senator Gore, of Oklahoma, has twice introduced a resolution declaring that those voting for Representatives, Senators, *and President* shall have the qualifications requisite for electors of the most numerous branch of the State legislatures.[9] A third resolution of his stipulated that only citizens of the United States should be entitled to vote for President, Representatives, and Senators.[10]

An amendment on this subject, introduced in 1921 by Mr. Hill, of New York, declared that aliens were not to be counted in adjusting the apportionment of Representatives among the States.[11]

In 1921 Mr. Montague, of Virginia, introduced an amendment providing that no person not a citizen of the United States shall have the right to vote for Senator, Representative, or electors for President and Vice President.[12]

---

[8]App., No. 174.
[9]App., No. 861.
[10]App., No. 1011.
[11]App., No. 1035.
[12]App., No. 1046.

In January, 1927, Mr. Wilson, of Mississippi, offered a resolution declaring that foreign-born citizens of the United States shall not be eligible to the office of Senator or Representative.[13]

70. Japanese aliens.

The Japanese population in this country in 1920 was 110,010,[14] with the largest concentration thereof in the State of California. This State has had considerable difficulty in treating with them on account of their unequal competition with American workmen due to the fact that the standards of living of the two races are greatly different. In 1913 California passed a law prohibiting the holding of land by aliens ineligible to citizenship under United States law.[15] This effectually bars out Japanese subjects, for, under our naturalization laws, Japanese are not entitled to citizenship. But as Japanese children born in this country acquire American citizenship ipso facto (Fourteenth amendment, sec. 1), the intentions of the California land law have been frustrated in many cases by the transfer of the property in question to these new citizens.

In an attempt to repress this evasion of the law, an amendment was introduced on December 2, 1919, by Senator Jones, of Washington, declaring that children hereafter born of foreign parentage shall not be eligible "to citizenship in the United States unless both parents are eligible to become citizens of the United States."[16]

[13] App., No. 1304.

[14] World's Almanac, p. 711, census of 1920.

[15] Ogg, National Progress, p. 309.

[16] App., No. 1110.

Three days later Mr. Jones, of California, introduced the same amendment in the House of Representatives.[17] A similar resolution has been introduced five times since.[18] On January 21, 1920, Senator Phelan, of California, presented an amendment defining American citizenship as follows:

All persons born in the United States are subject to the jurisdiction thereof whose parents are white persons, Africans, American Indians, or their descendants, and all persons naturalized in the United States and subjects to the jurisdiction thereof are citizens of the United States and of the State wherein they reside.[19]

71. Excluding States from consideration of alien questions.

In order to avoid national embarrassment such as was caused in 1906 when California enforced a school regulation discriminating against Japanese and thus in supposed conflict with the rights guaranteed them by the treaty of 1894,[20] an amendment has been offered declaring that "Congress shall have the exclusive power to legislate on questions affecting the rights and privileges of citizens of other countries residing in the United States and the relations of the United States with other countries."[21] Along this same order Mr. Hulsten, of New York, has three times submitted an amendment designed to prohibit States from making laws discriminating against aliens with regard to holding property or enjoying all civil privileges and immunities.[22]

[17] App., No. 1009.

[18] App., Nos. 1057, 1153, 1156, 1173, 1267.

[19] App., No. 1012.

[20] Latane, America as a World Power, p. 299.

[21] App., No. 713.

[22] App., Nos. 874, 900, 989.

72. Religion.

In his message to Congress in 1875, President Grant suggested the adoption of an amendment declaring "the church and state forever separate and distinct, but each free within their proper spheres, and that all church property shall bear its own proportion of taxation."

Acting on this suggestion Mr. Blaine immediately introduced a resolution providing that "no State shall make any law respecting an establishment of religion or prohibiting the free exercise thereof," and it also prohibited the appropriation of public school money by any State to sectarian schools. This amendment passed the House but failed in the Senate, lacking the necessary two-thirds majority.[23]

Since then it has been reintroduced twenty times, but only once reported on by the committee to which referred,[24] which report recommended that the resolution do not pass. As most States, in their own constitutions, have prohibitions on this subject, a Federal amendment in this respect is hardly necessary.

One of the amendments mentioned above included the provision that "each State in this Union shall establish and maintain a system of free public schools adequate for the education of all the children living therein, between the ages of 6 and 16 years, inclusive, in the common branches of learning."[25] An amendment of this nature had been proposed nine times before. The first one was introduced by Mr. Delano, of Ohio, in 1865, and was in-

---

[23]Ames, p. 278.

[24]Ames, p. 278; App., Nos. 7, 157, 167, 191, 192, 210, 228, 259, 272, 325, 386, 421, 473, 830, 1287. No. 272 reported adversely.

[25]App., No. 7.

tended primarily to compel the Southern States to educate the freed negroes.[26] Most States now maintain comprehensive school systems and are improving on them regularly. There is but little need, therefore, for a Federal amendment compelling State action in this respect.

In 1921 and 1924, Mr. Upshaw, of Georgia, introduced two resolutions declaring that no law shall be passed respecting the establishment of religion, nor shall the National or any State Government or political subdivision thereof use public moneys for sectarian or ecclesiastical institutions.[27] A similar amendment was introduced in May, 1928, by Mr. Lowrey, of Mississippi.[28]

73. Recognizing the Deity in the Constitution.

Although many of the States that helped frame the Constitution had regularly established churches, and some of them made heresy a disqualification for office, yet all reference to any particular religion, or even the Deity itself, was purposely omitted from the organic law of the land, thus keeping state and church definitely apart.[29] There was even a doubt as to whether an oath should be required of Federal and State officers in their acknowledgment to support and defend the Constitution.[30]

In keeping with the proclaimed desire to be freed of those troubles which result from religious quarrels in government, of which there had been many eloquent examples in Europe, the fathers of the Constitution included therein the provision that " No religious test shall

[26] Ames, p. 276.

[27] App., Nos. 1075, 1232.

[28] App., No. 1361.

[29] Watson, David K. The Constitution, p. 1338.

[30] Ibid., p. 1333.

ever be required as a qualification to any office or public trust under the United States." (Art. VI, sec. 3.) The Constitution was therefore committed to a definite let-alone policy as regards religion, and carrying this principle into effect the United States declared in one of its early treaties that the United States was in no way founded upon the Christian religion.[31] As late as 1876, an amendment was proposed which excluded ministers of any denomination from holding office under the Government of the United States.[32]

Yet despite the fact that the Constitution remains silent regarding any national religion it is well recognized by all that the United States is a Christian nation,[33] and of late efforts have been made to incorporate a statement of this accepted fact into the Constitution. The first amendment on this subject was introduced by Mr. Frye, of Maine, in 1894, and provided that there should be added to the preamble the declaration that "We, the people of the United States, devoutly acknowledging the supreme authority and just government of God in all the affairs of men and nations, and grateful to Him for our civil and religious liberty; and encouraged by the assurances of His word, invoke His guidance, as a Christian nation, according to His appointed way, through Jesus Christ, in order to form," etc.[34] This amendment was reintroduced in the same year by Mr. Morse, of Massachusetts. and twice again by the same men in 1895.[35] In 1896 Mr. Willis, of

[31] Treaty with Morocco, 1787; Putney, Constitutional Law, p. 360.
[32] Watson, p. 1338.
[33] Bryce, American Commonwealth, II, p. 702.
[34] App., No. 142.
[35] App., Nos. 142, 143, 169, 170.

Delaware, submitted an amendment providing for the insertion of the phrase, " trusting in Almighty God," in the preamble between the phrases " our posterity " and " do ordain." [36] The last series of amendments in this field came in the 2-year period 1908–1910, and declared that the preamble should begin with the words " In the name of God." There were four such amendments.[37]

74. Proposition to change the name of the country.

Two amendments have been introduced to change the name of the country. The first one was presented by Mr. Anderson in 1866 and declared that in the event the Constitution was again to be amended the name of this Nation was hereafter to " be known and styled America." [38]

The other proposition was presented by Mr. Miller, of Wisconsin, and declared that " The name of this Republic is hereby changed from the United States of America to the United States of the Earth." This amendment contains many whimsical features, and since it was presented, as noted on the resolution itself, " by request," the sponsor may not have been responsible for any of its erratic provisions. One section reads: " The Army and Navy, including the Army and Navy schools of organized murder, are hereby abolished, and whenever the rights of the people can not be secured through the courts, then the President shall call out the militia of the several States," etc. Another section reads: " The House and Senate shall vote by electricity." Also, that " No law shall go into effect

[36] App., No. 195.
[37] App., Nos. 509, 516, 524, 565.
[38] Ames, p. 280.

or remain in effect that is not at all times demanded and sustained by a majority of the people whom it affects." All offices are made elective, and the initiative, referendum, and recall are liberally taken care of.[39]

75. Cumulative voting.

On February 1, 1917, Mr. Murray, of Oklahoma, proposed an amendment to the Constitution providing for cumulative voting. His plan is a unique one and provides that every citizen over 21 years of age shall be entitled to one vote with an extra vote for each of the following merits: Being married, being the head of a family with at least two minor children dependent upon him or her, having mastered a certain curriculum to be uniform throughout the United States, and having served in the Army or Navy against a foreign foe.[40] It is claimed by the author that under this system the home would become a greater unit of strength and that "families of the country would constitute the elective power of all candidates to public office. It is further claimed by Mr. Murray under his amendment that legislation would proportionately reflect the demands and interests of the country, and since homes are built among all classes it would tend to place a check upon class legislation based upon accommodations of wealth and poverty, but would go directly toward the object of fostering and building the home interest of the country." [41]

---

[39] App., No. 114. Some of these provisions I have treated in the sections covering the subjects mentioned.—*Author.*

[40] App., No. 870.

[41] Cong. Rec., 64th Cong. 2d sess., p. 269.

76. Fortunes.

The ease and rapidity with which extraordinarily large fortunes accumulate when once a leisurely competence has been secured has prompted some reformers in this country toward designing plans for limiting the wealth a person may possess. This is desirable, they claim, because the possession of too much wealth by any private individual is bound to work to the disadvantage of the masses. Further, it is maintained that, as great as are some of the fortunes in this country, they are yet only in their infancy, "and being transmitted practically incorporate and intact, these fortunes are in the process of redoubling, by compound interest and compound dividend, from the present hundreds of millions of dollars each into eventually thousands of millions of dollars each, already an offense against public policy, simple justice, and vital religion and common sense."[42]

In the endeavor to strike directly and decisively at these fortunes, three amendments have been submitted prohibiting the possession in the United States by any one person of a wealth exceeding $10,000,000, and giving the Federal Government power to confiscate any such surplus.[43]

Allied to the amendments mentioned above in the object to be attained, but professedly based upon morality as cause, is the amendment offered in 1914 by Mr. Morin, of Pennsylvania, empowering the several States and the United States to dispossess any citizen or combination of citizens of all "wealth, property, power, influence, or

[42] Preamble to H. J. Res. No. 104; App., No. 438.

[43] App., Nos. 378, 379, 438.

honor" gained through dishonesty.[44] He included this same proposition in another resolution presented in 1917 denying the Supreme Court the power to declare this law or any law unconstitutional.[45]

---

[44] App., No. 769.

[45] App., No. 869. See sec. 31.

Chapter V

PROCEDURE AS TO CONSTITUTIONAL AMENDMENTS

77. Early proposals on this subject.

The difficulties and delays encountered in amending the Constitution have led to the introduction of various measures designed to make the amendment of the Constitution an easier business than as now provided for by Article V. Movements in this direction have been especially prevalent during recent years, 18 amendments with this object in view having been presented since 1911.

Prior to 1911, although the matter was much discussed in Congress, especially during the consideration of other amendments to the Constitution, but very few resolutions exclusively directed to altering Article V were presented. In 1826, owing to the great number of amendments proposed to change the method of election of President, prompted by the defeat of Jackson in 1824, Mr. Herrick, of Maine, offered a resolution proposing to prohibit the introduction of amendments to the Constitution except in every tenth year.[1] In 1882 Mr. Berry, of California, recommended the adoption of an amendment providing that proposed amendments to the Constitution should be voted on by State legislatures which had been chosen, or the members of the most popular branch of which had been chosen next after the submission of the amendment, and at its first session.[2]

[1] Ames, p. 285.

[2] Ibid., pp. 288–290.

Of the thirteen original States Rhode Island was the last to ratify the Constitution. Her delay was due to the fear that the larger States, and the new States to be admitted, might by reason of their size completely overshadow her sovereign rights. As a protection in this respect she proposed an amendment that after 1793 no amendment to the Constitution should be made "without the consent of 11 of the States heretofore united under the Confederation." [3]

In 1864 and 1873 resolutions were proposed with the object of reducing the majority of the vote required to propose, and the majority in the number necessary to ratify, amendments. The first stipulated that amendments could be proposed by a majority of the Members elected to each House or a convention called on the application of the legislatures of a majority of the several States, and that two-thirds of the conventions or legislatures of the States, whichever method might be directed by Congress, could ratify. The other proposition was to the effect that "Congress, whenever three-fifths of both Houses of Congress deem it necessary, may propose amendments to the Constitution, or may call a convention for proposing amendments and revising the Constitution," and shall be required to call such a convention "on the application of the legislatures of any number of States, embracing three-fifths of the enumerated population of the several States."

Amendments under either of these methods were to be valid when approved and ratified by a majority of the electors in the several States voting thereon.[4]

[3] Ames, p. 292.

[4] Ibid., p. 293.

Another proposal calling for popular ratification of proposed amendments was that advanced by Mr. Davis, of Kentucky, in 1869, which provided that the fifteenth amendment, which was then under consideration, and all other amendments, should not become effective until favorably voted on by a majority of the people entitled to vote in three-fourths of the several States.[5]

78. Recent attempts to change Article V.

Although in recent years the attempts to alter Article V have been numerous, the methods suggested have also been numerous. In the 18 amendments on this subject introduced since 1911 there have been embodied almost as many different plans for effecting that change in the organic law, which it is generally recognized may be necessary as new conditions present themselves.

It is practically impossible to group these amendments so that they will fall into any few definitely limited classes. They differ from each other in so many features as to make it almost necessary to describe each one by itself. For convenience in treatment, however, I have in some measure divided them, but it must be understood that where an amendment is placed in one of the following sections this does not mean that it necessarily contains none of the features discussed in another section.

The first amendment of this series, which commenced in 1911, indicated that the author, Senator Bristow, of Kansas, felt that while ratification of a proposed amendment should be difficult, and therefore the system in that respect should remain as it is, the matter of proposal should be very simple. He therefore resolved that " when-

[5]Ames, p. 294.

ever the legislature of any State wishes the Constitution altered it shall pass a resolution embodying the proposed change or amendment and send a copy to the Secretary of State, who shall without delay transmit a copy thereof to the governor of every State with a request that it shall be brought before the State legislature either at the next regular session or at a special session, as the governor may think advisable."[6] In 1912, Mr. Jackson and, in 1914, Mr. Doolittle, both also of Kansas, introduced practically the same resolution.[7]

79. Changing majorities required for congressional proposals, calling of conventions, and ratifications.

On the contrary, Mr. Crumpacker, of Indiana, in 1913 introduced an amendment to make easier the ratification of proposed amendments. After stating that a majority of the Members of both Houses was sufficient to propose amendments and that on the application of two-thirds of the State legislatures Congress should call a convention, it went on to declare that ratification could be effected by the legislatures of two-thirds of the States containing a majority of the inhabitants of the United States or by convention in two-thirds thereof.[8]

An amendment of a somewhat similar nature was presented by Mr. Lafferty, of Oregon, in the same year, it differing from the preceding proposal only in that the will of a majority of the States was sufficient to call a convention, and that in the individual States the legislatures

[6]App., No. 578.
[7]App., Nos. 652, 747.
[8]App., No. 664.

could, if they desired, arrange for ratification by a direct vote of the people.[9]

Still carrying out the proposition that an absolute majority of both Houses of Congress should suffice for proposing amendments, Mr. Chandler, of New York, went further with regard to the calling of conventions and proposed in his resolution, introduced June 10, 1913, that one-fourth of the States, containing at least one-fourth of the population of the United States, were to have the authority to call a convention, and that the call by the States might be made by the legislatures thereof or by a vote of a majority of the electors voting thereon. The amendments proposed under either of these were to be submitted to the people, and " if in the majority of States a majority of the electors voting thereon approve the proposed amendments, and if the majority of all the electors voting thereon shall also approve the proposed amendments," they shall be considered ratified. This resolution also provided that Congress should call a constitutional convention in 1920, and one every 30 years thereafter.[10] Mr. Chandler reintroduced this proposal in 1916.[11]

Along this same order was the resolution introduced by Mr. MacGregor, of New York, in 1920, proposing that upon the application of the people of two-thirds of the States by a referendum of the electors of such States, Congress " shall call a convention for proposing amendments," and that amendments proposed by Congress or such convention " shall be valid to all intents and purposes as part

[9]App., No. 704.
[10]App., No. 717.
[11]App., No. 859.

of this Constitution when ratified by the people of three-fourths of the several States who shall express their approval or disapproval of the proposed amendment by a referendum vote of the electors of the several States." [12]

In 1911, 1924, 1926, and 1928, Mr. Berger, of Wisconsin, proposed an amendment stipulating that a constitutional convention could be convened on the affirmative vote to that effect of both Houses of Congress.[13]

80. Senator La Follette's plan.

Senator La Follette, of Wisconsin, twice sponsored resolutions designed to facilitate amendments to the Constitution. His plan provided that amendments may be proposed by a majority of both Houses of Congress or by resolutions adopted in the legislatures of 10 States, which proposals shall be submitted to the several States for ratification by the electors qualified to vote for the election of Representatives in Congress, the vote to be taken "at the next ensuing election of Representatives, in such manner as the Congress prescribes. If in a majority of the States a majority of the electors voting approve the proposed amendments, and if a majority of all the electors voting also approve the proposed amendment, they shall be valid to all intents and purposes as part of this Constitution." He introduced this resolution in 1912 and 1913.[14]

A simple and easy change of Article V was recommended by Mr. Thompson, of Kansas, in his resolution of 1913 declaring that a majority of both Houses of Con-

[12]App., No. 1019.
[13]App., Nos. 607, 1296, 1356.
[14]App., Nos. 650, 705.

gress and a majority of the legislatures of the States were sufficient to respectively propose and ratify amendments.[15]

81. Senator Owen's plan.

In 1911, 1913, 1915, 1917, 1921, and 1923, Senator Owen, of Oklahoma, introduced an amendment stipulating that a majority vote of both Houses be sufficient to propose amendments, and that a request from a majority of the States be sufficient authority for Congress to call a convention. If one of the Houses twice rejected the proposal made by the other, and three months' delay without favorable action was to be considered equivalent to a rejection, the proposing House could proceed as if it had the consent of the other. In the constitutional conventions Congress was to be permitted to submit competing measures.

The proposed amendments were to be voted on by the people throughout the States, and the returns of the election were to be counted by the House of Representatives. In such an election the vote of a double majority was to prevail—" a majority of those who vote on the measure in a majority of the congressional districts and a majority of all the votes cast thereon." Another unique feature of this plan was that the voters were to be furnished with a pamphlet containing the arguments for and against the contemplated amendment, the same to be prepared by two committees composed of leading representatives of the opposing sides.[16] Supporting his amendment introduced in 1915, Senator Owen introduced a bill (S. 1084) " to provide a direct, truthful, and inexpensive means of

[15]App., No. 677.
[16]App., Nos. 615, 699, 797, 894, 1053, 1191.

communication between the voters and candidates for nomination and election to certain Federal offices, and to provide publicity for amendments to the Federal Constitution submitted by Congress, and the reasons for and against their adoption." [17]

82. Senator Cummins's plan.

A plan which makes the amendment of the Constitution less difficult and yet does not go to any complicated democratic extreme is that which was recommended by Senator Cummins, of Iowa.[18] His plan only alters and adds to the present scheme by permitting the legislatures of 16 of the States to propose amendments, and two-thirds of the States, voting by people or legislature as the States direct, to ratify proposed amendments. The resolution embodying this plan was reported adversely by the Committee on the Judiciary February 5, 1914, but it appears that the adverse report was based upon an inability to agree on certain details. The minority of the committee filed an opinion in which they stated that although there was a difference about details, the committee was "of one mind in that there should be submitted to the States for approval or rejection an amendment providing that either a proportion of the States or a proportion of the people, or both, should have the power to initiate amendments to our Constitution." [19]

In 1915 Senator Cummins reintroduced this amendment with the additional provision that upon the presentation to the President of a petition of 15 per cent of

[17] App., No. 794.

[18] App., No. 708.

[19] S. Rept. No. 147, 63d Cong., 2d sess.

the voters in 24 States, the amendment should be considered formally proposed, and the President should submit it to the States for ratification.[20]

83. Initiative amendments.

On August 13, 1914, Mr. Igoe, of Missouri, introduced an amendment adding three new ways of proposing amendments to the Constitution: 1. On the petition of 10 per cent of the voters of a majority of the States asking for the submission of a certain amendment, such amendment should be voted upon in a national referendum. 2. Whenever a proposed amendment shall have passed both Houses of Congress, either House may arrange for its submission to the people for ratification. 3. Whenever a proposed amendment has passed both Houses of Congress, 10 per cent of the voters of the States may ask by petition for its submission to the people for ratification. In any of these cases if the amendment receives a majority of the votes in a majority of the States and a majority of the total votes in all the States, it shall be declared adopted.[21]

Mr. Bryan, of Washington, submitted for consideration on February 15, 1915, an amendment providing that a majority vote of both Houses shall be sufficient to propose amendments, and adding that—

> At the first presidential election following the adoption of this amendment, and at every fifth presidential election thereafter, and at such other presidential elections as a majority of Congress or a majority of the several States shall determine, the question "Shall there be a convention to propose amendments to the Constitution of the United States?" shall be submitted to the electors.

---

[20] App., No. 806.
[21] App., No. 763.

In the event of an affirmative majority vote, the delegates in number equal to each State's representation in Congress are to be chosen as the State legislatures respectively determine. This convention shall " propose amendments which shall be submitted to the electors, and if accepted by two-thirds of electors voting thereon " shall become part of the Constitution.[22]

In 1916 an amendment was presented adding to the present methods of proposing amendments that of two-thirds of the States submitting proposals through a majority vote of the electors therein. Ratification of proposed amendments could also be had through a majority vote of the electors in three-fourths of the States.[23]

In 1924 Mr. Boyland, of New York, proposed an amendment declaring that upon a majority vote of the people of two-thirds of the States to that effect, a convention should be called for the purpose of initiating amendments to the Constitution.[24]

Of all the propositions which declare for a more popular control over the adoption of new amendments that of Senator Pomerene, of Ohio, is probably the most democratic. Its provisions apply to laws as well as to amendments and declare that upon submission to the Secretary of State of a petition signed by 500,000 voters of the United States, asking for a proposed constitutional amendment or law, that official shall submit the question to the people at the next regular congressional election. If the petition is signed by 1,000,000 voters then a special election shall be called for determining a choice. The acceptance of the proposed constitutional amendment or

[22]App., No. 758.

[23]App., No. 851. Proposed by Mr. Gray, of Indiana.

[24]App., No. 1227.

law by a majority of the electorate will make it effective.[25] An identical proposition was presented by Mr. Emerson, of Ohio, in 1919, by Mr. Morin, of Pennsylvania, in 1921, and by Mr. Dyer, of Missouri, in 1928.[26]

84. Ratification by popular vote.

It was undoubtedly the agitation which surrounded the passage of the woman suffrage and prohibition amendments, either or both of which measures affect directly nearly every home in the country, that prompted the submission of most of the propositions declaring for a popular ratification of all proposed amendments. Nineteen such resolutions were introduced in Congress between 1917 and 1928.[27] Two of these, both introduced by Senator Brandegee, of Connecticut, left it to Congress to determine whether the ratification should be by legislatures or the electorate.[28]

An amendment introduced by Mr. Juul, of Illinois, in 1919 provided that the ratification of proposed amendments should continue to be by State legislatures, but that the vote of each State should be in units identical with its voting strength in the electoral college; that is, it should be allowed as many votes as it has Representatives and Senators in Congress, and that three-fourths of this combined voting strength should be required for ratification.[29]

A proposition which has of late been much discussed is that all proposed amendments should be ratified by

[25] App., No. 994.

[26] App., Nos. 996, 1067, 1350.

[27] App., Nos. 926, 933, 966, 1007, 1015, 1044, 1045, 1048, 1063, 1067, 1071, 1076, 1164, 1165, 1175, 1180, 1227, 1243, 1263.

[28] App., Nos. 926, 933.

[29] App., No. 1006.

State legislatures, at least one house of which shall have been elected subsequent to the date of the proposal of said amendment. Mr. Garrett, of Tennessee, introduced two such amendments in the Sixty-seventh and one each in the Sixty-eighth, Sixty-ninth, and Seventieth Congresses.[30] In the Senate, Senator Wadsworth, of New York, introduced similar amendments in the Sixty-seventh, Sixty-eighth, and Sixty-ninth Congresses.[31]

Mr. Garrett's resolution, introduced in the Sixty-eighth Congress (H. J. Res. No. 68), was considered by the Committee on the Judiciary, to which it was referred, hearings were held, and it was favorably reported back to the House on June 3, 1924.

That a constitutional amendment is necessary in order to effect the change outlined in this amendment was made evident by the decision of the Supreme Court in the case of Hawke *v.* Smith.[32] Here the State of Ohio had, in accordance with a provision in its State constitution that "the people also reserve to themselves the legislative power of the referendum on the action of the general assembly ratifying any proposed amendment to the Constitution of the United States," held a State referendum on the question of approving the ratification of the eighteenth amendment after the State legislature had already accepted it.

A petition was filed for a writ of injunction seeking to restrain the secretary of state from spending public money in preparing and printing forms of the ballot for use in the referendum election. It was demurred to and the demurrer sustained by all the courts of Ohio. The case

[30] App., Nos. 1060, 1140, 1187, 1260, 1343.
[31] App., Nos. 1055, 1175, 1271.
[32] 253 U. S. 221.

was carried to the Supreme Court of the United States, which reversed the Ohio courts, saying: " The function of a State legislature in ratifying a proposed amendment to the Federal Constitution, like the function of Congress in proposing such amendment, is a Federal function, derived not from the people of that State, but from the United States Constitution." [33]

Mr. Garrett's resolution, as also Senator Wadsworth's, contained the further proposition that a State may require that the act of ratification by its legislature be subject to confirmation by popular vote. This feature was criticized by Mr. Griffin, of New York, who claimed that under its provisions, if an amendment were defeated by the legislatures no recourse to the people was possible, whereas if it were accepted its opponents still had an opportunity to appeal to the people, if the legislatures so directed. Further, it would impose on the State legislatures the responsibility whether a constitutional amendment should be passed upon by them finally, or by the people, and the result " will ever remain open to argument and dissatisfaction." [34]

Mr. Garrett's resolution did not reach a vote.

Senator Wadsworth's amendment, which was introduced in the Senate on December 6, 1923, was reported back from the Committee on the Judiciary with an amendment which completely changed the scope of the original proposal. For ratification by the legislatures it substituted ratification by the people.[35]

Senator Ashurst, of Arizona, spoke in favor of ratification by the people, declaring there is no State in the

[33] 253 U. S. 221.

[34] Cong. Rec., vol. 66, pt. 4, p. 4206.

[35] Cong. Rec., vol. 65, pt. 4, p. 3675.

Federal Union whose constitution may be amended by the State legislature. "If the consent of the voters in every State be required, and they are actually required, to alter and amend a State constitution, a fortiori the vote of citizens should be required to amend the Federal Constitution. Every argument in favor of election of Senators by a direct vote of the people is a stronger argument in favor of consulting the people on constitutional amendments." [36]

Senator Brandegee, of Connecticut, advanced the interesting observation that "inasmuch as the people will not allow their own State constitutions to be amended without a reference to the electors of their own States, the present system of amending the United States Constitution vitiates that protection, because when we amend the United States Constitution without going to the electors of the States, but only to the legislatures, the United States Constitution having been amended, ipso facto it amends the constitution of every State; so that indirectly the States are now allowing their own constitutions to be amended in ways they themselves have prohibited." [37]

Senator Borah, of Idaho, commenting on the proposed resolution, stated that there would be no special merit in requiring one house of the ratifying legislature to have been elected after the constitutional amendment was proposed, for the reason that "in all probability the legislatures would be elected upon different issues, and therefore we would not get a true expression of the people upon this one proposition." [38]

Senator Jones, of Washington, submitted an amendment to the resolution providing that the vote of every

---

[36] Cong. Rec., vol. 65, pt. 4, p. 3675.

[37] Ibid., p. 3676.

[38] Cong. Rec., Mar. 30, 1924, vol. 65, pt. 4, p. 4563.

legislature acting on a proposed Federal constitutional amendment shall then be passed upon by the people of the State involved. It was claimed in support of this amendment that this would give the legislature an opportunity to discuss the measure, and thus bring its various features, recommendations, and criticisms to the attention of the people.[39]

Senator Walsh, of Montana, opposed to the Jones amendment, was of the opinion that when the action of the legislature is merely academic, as it would be under the amendment, there is very little likelihood that it will be debated in the legislature with any degree of interest or concern.[40] Further, that such activity would defer the ratification of an amendment to the Constitution by at least two years. Senator Brandegee was of the opinion that a little delay would be a good thing.[41] Senator McKellar, of Tennessee, declared himself opposed to the amendment, as it would render the resolution cumbersome.[42] Some Senators, opposed to the insertion of the Jones amendment, declared nevertheless they would vote for it if necessary in order to get the necessary two-thirds vote to pass the resolution, and it thus eventually was agreed upon.[43]

This amendment, however, was evidently accepted with some misgiving, for on the next day Senator Dial, of South Carolina, moved its reconsideration. This was agreed to, and upon a motion to strike out it was stricken from the resolution on a vote of 39 yeas to 35 nays.[44]

---

[39] Cong. Rec., Mar. 30, 1924, vol. 65, pt. 4, p. 4802.

[40] Ibid., p. 4931.

[41] Ibid., p. 4934.

[42] Ibid., p. 4940.

[43] Ibid., pp. 4938–4940.

[44] Ibid., p. 5003.

Further debate on the resolution and its conflicting amendments brought the Senate around to the point where it received with approbation the suggestion of Senator Swanson, of Virginia, that the entire matter be referred back to the Committee on the Judiciary for further consideration and report. Upon a motion to recommit the vote was 41 yeas and 28 nays.[45]

85. Length of time in which ratification may be made.

As the Constitution is silent as to the period during which a State may act upon a proposed amendment, it is a mooted question whether amendments once proposed remain acceptable until definitely accepted, or, even if rejected, are still open to ratification if sufficient rejecting States change their votes. It has been argued that an amendment may be submitted " for a thousand years and be in force when ratified." [46] Acting on this theory, the Senate of Ohio adopted a resolution in 1873 ratifying the second of the 12 amendments submitted to the States by Congress in 1789, but then rejected.[47]

In a speech in the Senate on February 28, 1924, Senator Ashurst, of Arizona, pointed out that at the time he was speaking there were four different amendments pending before the States for action.[48]

It is contended now that the child-labor amendment, although rejected by 13 States, is still before the States

[45] Cong. Rec., Mar. 30, 1924, vol. 65, pt. 4, p. 5009.

[46] Discussion on S. J. Res. 90, 65th Cong. 2d sess. Cong. Rec., pp. 8612, 10098.

[47] Cong. Rec., vol. 55, pt. 6, p. 5558, quoting Jameson, Constitution, pp. 634–636.

[48] Amendments proposed, respectively, Sept. 15, 1789, Sept. 15, 1789, May 1, 1810, and Mar. 2, 1861.

for ratification as enough rejecting States may change their votes to bring about ratification.[49]

The first resolution seeking to amend the Constitution so as to provide a limit to the offering period was presented by Senator Chilton of West Virginia. The limit designated by this resolution was five years.[50] Ten others have been presented since then with the periods in question ranging from five to eight years.[51]

The eighteenth amendment is the only amendment actually adopted which carried within its own provisions the time limit during which it might be ratified. Many of the constitutional amendments proposed since add a clause providing that unless the amendment is adopted within a certain number of years by the required number of ratifying States, it shall become inoperative. The power of Congress to append this time limit was questioned in the case of Dillon *v.* Gloss,[52] but the Supreme Court held such addition proper, declaring:

1. Article V of the Constitution implies that amendments submitted thereunder must be ratified, if at all, within some reasonable time after their proposal.
2. Under this article Congress, in proposing an amendment, may fix a reasonable time for ratification.
3. The period of seven years, fixed by Congress in the resolution proposing the eighteenth amendment was reasonable.

CHANGING VOTES ON RATIFICATION OR REJECTION

In the matter of ratifying or rejecting proposed amendments, another question of extreme importance arises,

[49] See sec. 51.
[50] App., No. 751.
[51] App., Nos. 870, 924, 925, 926, 933, 960, 1063, 1076, 1175, 1243.
[52] 256 U. S. 368.

may a State, having once voted on a proposed amendment, change its vote?

It is generally accepted that a State which has said "no" may change and say "yes," but that a State having once voted "yes" may not change to "no." [53]

Senator Ashurst, however, is of the contrary opinion, declaring, "It is my opinion, after considerable research, that a State may at any time change its vote upon a ratification of a proposed amendment, provided the vote which it previously cast was not determinative of the result." [54]

In an effort definitively to settle this question, 10 resolutions submitted so far have contained provisions that until three-fourths of the States shall have ratified, or more than one-fourth of the States have rejected, a proposed amendment, any State may change its vote.[55] Two of these amendments contained the further provision that "if at any time more than one-fourth of the States have rejected the proposed amendment, said rejection shall be final and further consideration thereof by States shall cease." [56]

An amendment introduced by Senator Wadsworth, of New York, in 1921 carried the interesting provision that "when any amendment shall be rejected or defeated in more than one-fourth of the several States, the same may not be again proposed within two years." [57]

[53] 68th Cong., H. Doc. No. 570, p. 20.

[54] Cong. Rec., Mar. 6, 1924 (vol. 65, pt. 4, p. 3675).

[55] App., Nos. 1060, 1063, 1140, 1175, 1180, 1187, 1243, 1260, 1271, 1343.

[56] App., Nos. 1175, 1243.

[57] App., No. 1055.

CHAPTER VI

AMENDMENTS XIV TO XIX

86. The fourteenth amendment.

The freeing of the negro by the thirteenth amendment was intended to confer upon him the right of suffrage as well as the other civic rights of the white. Shortly after the termination of the Civil War the Southern States did grant the suffrage to the negroes, but, as the right was a revocable one, it was soon evident that in order to assure them a continuation of this right some form of a constitutional protection was necessary. Accordingly, the fourteenth amendment was made to include the provision that the basis of a State's representation in Congress would be decreased in the proportion which the number of disfranchised citizens bore to the whole number of citizens. Congress did not pass any law providing for the enforcement of this provision and, as the guarantee of the suffrage was only a negative one, two years later the fifteenth amendment was adopted affirmatively guaranteeing the negro against the deprivation of his vote.

The guarantees above mentioned were circumvented by the Southern States through the application of certain educational and property tests which the negroes were little able to meet. The educational test has been declared constitutional because while it deprives the negro of his vote, the deprivation does not come about on account of his race.[1] With these tests in effect, supplemented by the so-called "grandfather clause," the Southern States have succeeded in keeping the negro voteless without endangering the vote of the white.[2]

They have not, however, in accordance with section 2 of the fourteenth amendment, reduced their representation in Congress. As the negro was only counted as three-fifths of a man before the war, and as a whole man after the adoption of the thirteenth amendment, the Southern States have thus secured a larger delegation in Congress and a bigger vote in the Electoral College than when the negro was a slave. It was estimated that in 1884, when the Democrats were successful at the polls, they secured 24 seats in Congress and cast 38 votes in the Electoral College to which they were not entitled.[3] In the election of 1888 the average vote cast for a Member in Congress in 5 Southern States was less than 8,000, whereas in 5 Northern States it was over 36,000. In an effort to remedy this anomalous situation the Republicans in Congress in 1890 introduced a bill providing for Federal supervision over all Federal elections. The measure was referred to as the " Force Bill " and passed the House, but failed in the Senate.[4]

Under the apprehension that Congress might at some time pass some measure enforcing the decreased representation called for by the action of section 2 of the four-

[1] Williams *v.* Mississippi (170 U. S. 222).

[2] Hall, J. P., Constitutional Law, p. 80. See also Collins, C. W. The Fourteenth Amendment, Chapter VI, Results to the Negro Race, pp. 63–80.

[3] Dewey, D. R., National Problems, p. 162.

[4] Ibid., p. 170.

teenth amendment, nine attempts have been made to repeal all of section 2 but the first sentence.[5] Two other resolutions provided for the repeal of the entire fourteenth amendment.[6] With the exception of one,[7] all these resolutions were introduced by Representatives from the South. Mr. Hardwick, of Georgia, was the most active of these introducers, having presented seven such resolutions from 1903 to 1913.

The last two proposals to effect a change in the fourteenth amendment were in no way connected with the original purpose of that amendment. A resolution presented by Senator Jones, of Washington, in 1914 was designed to bring about applied representative government and declared that " Representatives shall be apportioned among the several States according to their respective number of electors vocationally. But when the right to vote," etc.[8] An amendment by Senator Poindexter, introduced in 1919, was intended to accomplish universal woman suffrage by amending the fourteenth amendment by striking out the word " male."[9]

87. The fifteenth amendment.

The same reasons that prompted southern delegates to attempt the repeal of section 2 of the fourteenth amendment have also led them to attempt to repeal the fifteenth amendment itself, the root of the trouble. From 1900 to 1915, 23 resolutions were introduced calling for the repeal

[5] App., Nos. 395, 424, 439, 469, 492, 601, 605, 622, 701.

[6] App., Nos. 533, 673.

[7] App., No. 439 (introduced by Mr. Smith, of Pennsylvania).

[8] App., No. 750.

[9] App., No. 987.

of the fifteenth amendment.[10] Six of these were introduced by Senator Underwood, of Alabama, five by Mr. Kitchin, of North Carolina, and five by Mr. Hardwick, of Georgia.

It is apparent that all these efforts must be in vain, for it is hardly possible that a three-fourths majority of the States can be secured to repeal the fifteenth amendment and any part of the fourteenth amendment, representing, as they do, the fruit of the Civil War, which cost the country so much blood and treasure.[11]

88. Income tax amendment.

The revenue act of 1894 provided, among other things, that—

> There shall be assessed, levied, collected, and paid annually upon the gains, profits, and income received in the preceding calendar year by every citizen of the United States, whether residing at home or abroad, and every person residing therein, whether said gains, profits, or income be derived from any kind of property, rents, interest, dividends, or salaries, or from any profession, trade, employment, or vocation carried on in the United States or elsewhere, or from any other source whatever, a tax of two per centum on the amount so derived over and above four thousand dollars, and a like tax shall be levied, collected, and paid annually upon the gains, profits, and income from all property owned and of every business, trade, or profession carried on in the United States by persons residing without the United States.[12]

In the famous case of Pollock *v.* Farmers' Loan & Trust Co.[13] the Supreme Court in two decisions declared that,

[10] App., Nos. 305, 313, 324, 354, 385, 393, 394, 414, 422, 425, 464, 470, 474, 491, 499, 534, 537, 542, 602, 622, 673, 702, 791.

[11] Bryce, Vol. II, p. 511.

[12] Sec. 27, 28 Stat., 509, ch. 349.

[13] 157 U. S. 429; 158 U. S. 601.

firstly, taxes on real estate being direct taxes, taxes on rents or income therefrom are also direct taxes; secondly, that taxes on personal property or on the income therefrom are direct taxes; and that finally as these taxes were not apportioned in accordance with Article I, section 2, clause 3, and Article I, section 9, clause 4, of the Constitution, that part of the law providing for their collection was repugnant to the Constitution and therefore void.

As the final decision was given by a divided court, 5 to 4, with the minority writing vigorous dissenting opinions, the judgment of the court, although no less effective in declaring the law in question unconstitutional, was quite generally criticized.[14] This was especially due to the fact that income tax laws had been passed before and declared constitutional. From 1861 to 1870 nine laws involving the taxation of rentals from real estate, products of personal property, and the profits of business or profession, were passed. None of these were invalidated by the courts.[15]

It was seriously considered by many legal authorities that the Supreme Court might modify its decision in considering another case on the subject, and, if not this, new members coming into the court would seek its reversal.[16] On this supposition the Democratic Party included in

[14] See Discussion, Cong. Rec., vol. 44, pt. 4, pp. 4105–4121, 4390–4441.

[15] 157 U. S., 626 (Justice White).

[16] This was based on the fact that a line of decisions running from 1794 had clearly indicated that an income tax was not prohibited by the Federal Constitution. Hylton *v.* U. S., 3 Dallas; Veazie Bank *v.* Fenn, 8 Wall. 533; Pacific Insurance Co. *v.* Soule, 7 Wall. 433; Springer *v.* U. S., 102 U. S. 586.

their platform of 1896, after declaring their adherence to the principle of an income tax: [17]

> We declare that it is the duty of Congress to use all the constitutional power which remains after that decision or which may come by its reversal by the court as it may hereafter be constituted, so that the burdens of taxation may be equally and impartially laid, to the end that wealth may bear its due proportion of the expenses of the Government.

Although there was a strong public opinion that there was nothing in the Constitution which forbade the levying of an income tax by the Federal Government, in spite of the Supreme Court's decision, yet as that decision had become the supreme law of the land it had to be respected as such. So long as that decision stood Congress had no power to enact an income tax. Accordingly, to remove all doubt on the question and put it forever to rest, legislators began to propose an amendment to the Constitution specifically declaring the power of Congress in this field. Mr. Butler, of North Carolina, was the first to propose such an amendment, which he did on December 27, 1895.[18] The next year two more on the subject were presented,[19] and in 1897 there were six.[20] From then until 1909, 33 attempts were made to override the Supreme Court's decision by a constitutional amendment.[21]

The conviction entertained by many that another income tax law passed by Congress might be favorably considered by the Supreme Court doubtlessly delayed favorable action on the amendment. In his message to Con-

---

[17] Bloom, S. S. American Democracy, pp. 109–110.

[18] App., No. 177.

[19] App., Nos. 182, 200.

[20] App., Nos. 213, 217, 220, 222, 224, 227.

[21] See Appendix.

gress on December 4, 1906, President Roosevelt, touching this subject, said: [22]

The question is undoubtedly very intricate, delicate, and troublesome. The decision of the court was only reached by 1 majority. It is the law of the land, and is, of course, accepted as such and loyally obeyed by all good citizens. Nevertheless, the hesitation evidently felt by the court as a whole in coming to a conclusion, when considered together with the previous decisions on the subject, may perhaps indicate the possibility of devising a constitutional income tax law which shall substantially accomplish the result aimed at. The difficulty of amending the Constitution is so great that only real necessity can justify a resort thereto. Every effort should be made in dealing with this subject, as with the subject of the proper control by the National Government over the use of corporate wealth in interstate business, to devise legislation which without such action shall attain the desired end; but if this fails, there will ultimately be no alternative to a constitutional amendment.

An income-tax provision was prepared by Senators Bailey and Cummins to be added to the Payne tariff bill of 1909, but at the last moment it was substituted for a corporation-tax amendment.[23]

Finally on June 28, 1909, the Committee on Finance reported to the Senate a resolution proposing an amendment to the Constitution giving Congress "power to lay and collect taxes on incomes, from whatever source derived, without apportionment among the several States and without regard to any census or enumeration." [24] Senator McLaurin, of Mississippi, asserted that instead of an addition to, a subtraction from the Constitution was what was needed. All the trouble started by the Supreme Court over income taxes he declared was due to six words in the

[22] Messages and Papers of the Presidents, Vol. XVI, p. 7044.

[23] Cong. Rec., vol. 44, pt. 4, p. 4412.

[24] App., No. 540.

Constitution—" and direct taxes," appearing in the clause " Representatives and direct taxes shall be apportioned among the several States " (Art. I, sec. 2, cl. 3), and " or other direct " in the clause " No capitation or other direct tax shall be laid." (Art. I, sec. 9, cl. 2.) He therefore moved an amendment to strike out these words from the Constitution.[25] The amendment was not accepted. Senator Bailey, of Texas, moved to amend the resolution by adding after the word " incomes," " and may grade the same." He introduced also another amendment declaring that the proposed constitutional amendment be ratified by conventions in the respective States rather than by legislatures. This latter amendment was rejected, but the first one he withdrew, directly before the vote that was to be taken on same, explaining that he was certain it would be voted down, and he did not wish the Supreme Court to be able to say that " a proposition to authorize Congress to levy a graduated income tax was rejected." [26] The resolution itself was easily passed by a vote of 77 yeas to 15 nays.[27]

On July 12, 1909, the House took up the consideration of the Senate resolution and after a debate of four hours overwhelmingly passed it, 318 yeas to 14 nays. A great many of the speakers declared themselves opposed to the decision of the Supreme Court, but since there was no alternative they were compelled to accept its mandate and thus add an amendment to the Constitution which, ac-

[25] Cong. Rec., vol. 44, pt. 4, p. 4109.

[26] Senator Bailey explained that his amendment would be voted down not on its merits, but entirely on political grounds. Cong. Rec., vol. 44, pt. 4, p. 4120.

[27] Cong. Rec., vol. 44, pt. 4, p. 4121.

cording to the original order of things, they did not think was necessary.[28]

The amendment was proposed to the legislatures of the several States on the same day it passed the House, and on February 25, 1913, the Secretary of State issued an announcement to the effect that 38 of the 48 States had ratified it.[29]

89. Direct election of Senators.

In the Constitutional Convention four main plans for the selection of Senators were discussed: (1) Selection by the House of Representatives; (2) by the President; (3) election by the direct vote of the people; (4) by the legislatures of the several States. The first three plans were generally objected to on the grounds that No. 1 would make the Senate a dependency, No. 2 would be a step in the direction of monarchical government, and No. 3 would lead to confusion and clashes between the agricultural and manufacturing or commercial interests. The fourth plan offered the least objections and was unanimously accepted by the convention.[30]

The United States Senate has always commanded the respect of the world, and has indeed become the most effective and useful second chamber in existence.[31] Generally, therefore, comments on its work have been commendatory rather than otherwise. During the last quar-

[28] Document No. 12, 63d Cong., 1st sess., p. 56.

[29] Constitution of the United States, S. Doc. No. 154, 68th Cong., 1st sess., p. 31.

[30] Watson, David K. The Constitution of the United States, pp. 224–241.

[31] Bryce, The American Commonwealth, Vol. I, pp. 108–114.

ter of the nineteenth century, however, the movement for the popular election of Senators, which had been quite negligible before, developed into an emphatic demand that the Constitution be amended to bring about this reform. Charges were made, not exactly that the Senate was inefficient, but that under the system of indirect election through the State legislatures many of its members were indifferent to the popular demands of the day and more subservient to corporate interests whose corrupt influences made their election possible. There were, of course, no general accusations against the entire membership in this regard, but the disclosure of a few incidents where the members of legislatures had been subjected to monetary offers by interests working in the behalf of certain senatorial candidates very naturally led to the suspicion that there were other such cases not brought to light, and that at any rate the temptations for such malpractices should be removed by changing the method of election.[32]

Another objection to the choice of Senators by legislatures was that frequently a State went unrepresented or only half represented in the United States Senate on account of the inability of the legislature to agree on any one candidate. There were many cases where legislatures

[32] In the Sixty-second Congress a special committee was appointed to investigate charges that bribes had been used in the election of William Lorimer from Illinois. (Cong. Rec., p. 1490, vol. 47, pt. 2.) In the same Congress Senator Penrose made the statement that he had been offered one or two million dollars by Mr. Quinn, of Pennsylvania, to favor his candidacy in the legislature of Pennsylvania for election to the United States Senate. (Cong. Rec., vol. 48, pt. 11, p. 11467.) In the Forty-ninth Congress it was charged bribes had been used in the Legislature of Ohio to elect Payne to the Senate. (Rept. No. 1490, 49th Cong.)

were so deadlocked that balloting was carried on for months before a choice could be effected.[33]

Further, it was claimed by the supporters of the direct-election plan that the trend of the times the world over was toward a greater responsibility of government to the people. That " the nearer a governmental agency is to the source of power the greater will be its value, probity and efficiency. Direct responsibility results in honesty, and good faith sustains the wavering, lends encouragement to the timid, and exposes and defeats the unworthy, incompetent, and corrupt.[34]

That there was a popular demand for the direct election of Senators was also shown by pointing out that many of the States had taken the matter into their own hands by providing for primary elections which acted in the nature of a command to the particular legislature to elect the candidate for whom the greatest preference had been shown by the people.[35] By April, 1911, at least 31 States had declared by resolution or otherwise in favor of the direct-election principle.[36]

On the other side it was declared that there was no need for a constitutional amendment on this subject. That the existing method of election had brought to the Senate most of the greatest statesmen in American history, and that any modern inconvenience of delay which had crept into the time-honored method could easily be remedied by an act of Congress. Touching this matter Senator Root, of New York, a vigorous opponent of the idea of a change in the method of election, introduced in

[33] Bryce, vol. 1, p. 95.
[34] Cong. Rec., vol. 47, pt. 1, p. 208. Mr. Adair, of Indiana.
[35] Ibid., p. 211.
[36] H. Rept. No. 2, 62d Cong., 1st sess.

the Sixty-first and again in the Sixty-second Congress a bill providing that if a State legislature was unable to agree by majority vote on a certain candidate for the Senate within 20 days after the first convening of its two houses, then a plurality vote should govern. This would prevent a senatorial seat from remaining vacant for an indefinite length of time on account of a deadlock in one of the legislatures.[37] It was also argued that if an amendment was passed giving the people the right to elect Senators, the next step would be to apportion the number of Senators according to the population of the respective States, the same as Representatives. Of course, Article V guarantees every State two Senators, but this, it was pointed out, could be abolished itself by an amendment to that effect.[38]

90. Amendments introduced to effect popular election of Senators.

Previous to 1872 only nine resolutions on this subject had been introduced in Congress, the first one having been presented in 1826 by Mr. Storrs, of New York.[39] In 1872 two such amendments were offered; in 1873, three; in 1874, four; 1875 passed without one proposal on the subject, but the two succeeding years brought two each. Another gap came between 1877 and 1881 when, with but the exception of 1883, amendments were introduced every year ranging in number from but one presented in 1894, and that by Mr. Bryan, of Nebraska, to 26 in 1911, the year of the successful passage of the amendment.[40] In

[37] Cong. Rec., vol. 47, pt. 2, p. 1485.

[38] Ibid., 1486.

[39] Ames, p. 61.

[40] See Appendix.

all, there were 198 proposals,[41] 5 of which came to a vote. The measure came to a vote for the first time on July 21, 1894, passing the House by a vote of 141 yeas, 50 nays.[42] On January 12, 1898, it again was favorably voted upon by the House, 185 yeas, 11 nays.[43] By a vote of 242 yeas to 15 nays the proposition was passed for the third time by the House on April 13, 1900,[44] and the fourth time January 21, 1902, it passed without a recorded vote.[45] On February 28, 1911, it came to a vote in the Senate for the first time and failed of the two-thirds majority, the vote being 54 yeas, 33 nays.[46]

91. The seventeenth amendment.

The proposal which eventually became the seventeenth amendment was introduced in the House of Representatives by Mr. Rucker, of Missouri, on April 5, 1911. In its first stages it read as follows:

Resolved by the Senate and House of Representatives, etc., That in lieu of the first paragraph of section 3 of Article I of the Constitution of the United States and in lieu of so much of paragraph 2 of the same section as relates to any authority in Congress to make or alter regulations as to the times or manner of holding elections for Senators, the following be proposed as an amendment to the Constitution, which shall be valid to all intents and purposes as part of the Constitution when ratified by the legislatures of three-fourths of the States:

The Senate of the United States shall be composed of two Senators from each State, elected by the people thereof, for six years; and each Senator shall have one vote. The electors in each State shall

[41]Ames, pp. 61–63; see Appendix.

[42]App., No. 121.

[43]App., No. 226.

[44]App., No. 261.

[45]App., No. 334.

[46]App., No. 577.

have the qualifications requisite for electors of the most numerous branch of the State legislatures.

The times, places, and manner of holding elections for Senators shall be as prescribed in each State by the legislature thereof.

When vacancies happen in the representation of any State in the Senate, the executive authority of such State shall issue writs of election to fill such vacancies: *Provided,* That the legislature of any State may empower the executive thereof to make temporary appointments until the people fill the vacancies by election, as the legislature may direct.

This amendment shall not be so construed as to affect the election or term of any Senator chosen before it becomes valid as part of the Constitution.[47]

In addition to directing the popular election of Senators, it will be observed that this resolution proposed to change section 4 of Article I of the Constitution by taking away from Congress the power and the right to legislate in regard to the election of United States Senators, and give such control entirely and exclusively to the respective States. There was a practical unanimity on the proposal to elect Senators by popular vote, and not a Member of the House made any speech against its acceptance.

An opposition of some strength, however, arrayed itself against the proposition of denying Congress the right to supervise senatorial elections should it desire to interpose, and it was declared this provision would once more bring up the sectional issue.[48] Mr. Cannon, of Illinois, went so far as to state it was his opinion that this provision applied to the election of Representatives as well as to Senators, and that thus with Congress deprived of all power to enforce Federal elections, the States could ac-

[47] App., No. 592.

[48] Cong. Rec., vol. 47, pt. 1, p. 215.

complish the dissolution of Congress itself.[49] Mr. Young, of Michigan, immediately moved an amendment that "The times, places, and manner of holding elections for Senators and Representatives shall be prescribed in each State by the legislatures thereof; but the Congress may at any time by law make or alter such regulations, except as to the places of choosing Senators." [50]

Those in favor of the original resolution opposed Mr. Young's amendment on the ground that it would deprive the States of the right to prescribe the qualifications of voters in the election of Senators—a fundamental principle on which the Union was founded. Further, it was shown that this same resolution had been passed by the House three times before and would have probably been accepted by the Senate during the last session were it not for the addition in that body of what was known as the "Sutherland amendment," of which the Young amendment appeared to be an exact duplicate.[51]

Considerable debate centered around Young's amendment and it was finally rejected, 123 yeas to 189 nays.[52] A substitute offered by Mr. Mondell, which provided that "a plurality of the votes cast for candidates for Senator shall elect," was also defeated.[53] The resolution itself passed the House April 13 by a vote of 296 yeas to 16 nays.[54]

The Senate Committee on Judiciary, to which the resolution was now referred, reported it favorably to the Sen-

[49] Cong. Rec., vol. 47, pt. 1, p. 213.

[50] Ibid., p. 207.

[51] Cong. Rec., vol. 47, pt. i, p. 234.

[52] Ibid., p. 241.

[53] Ibid., p. 242.

[54] Ibid., p. 243.

ate, but a minority of the committee headed by Senator Sutherland presented practically the same objections which had prompted the Young amendment in the House, and which indeed in the preceding session Senator Sutherland himself had voiced in an amendment which bore his name. The opinion filed by the minority vigorously put forward the reasons for the preservation of the supervisory power conferred upon Congress by section 4 of Article I of the Constitution, and in support quoted Mr. Justice Miller in the decision rendered in the Yarbrough case: [55]

> If this Government is anything more than a mere aggregation of delegated agents of other States and governments, each of which is superior to the General Government, it must have the power to protect the elections on which its existence depends from violence and corruption. * * *
>
> If it has not this power it is left helpless before the two great natural and historical enemies of all republics—open violence and insidious corruption.
>
> If the Government of the United States has within its constitutional domain no authority to provide against these evils, if the very sources of power may be poisoned by corruption or controlled by violence and outrage, without legal restraint, then indeed is the country in danger, and its best powers, its highest purposes, the hopes which it inspires, and the love which enshrines it are at the mercy of the combinations of those who respect no right but brute force on the one hand and unprincipled corruptionists on the other.

In the Senate, Senator Bristow, of Kansas, immediately moved to amend the House resolution in accordance with the objections voiced by the minority of the committee. His amendment was merely to change section 2 of Article I of the Constitution to read "elected by the people thereof," instead of "chosen by the legislature thereof,"

[55] 110 U. S. 651; S. Rept. No. 35, 62d Cong., 1st sess.

and that senatorial electors "shall have the qualifications requisite for electors of the most numerous branch of the State legislature," and make the same provisions with regard to vacancies in the Senate as already apply to vacancies in the House of Representatives, adding the proviso that "The legislature of any State may empower the executive thereof to make temporary appointments until the people fill the vacancies by election as the legislature may direct." [56]

After a great deal of debate similar to the House debate on the same subject, the Bristow amendment was voted upon, and it passed the Senate on June 12, 1911, by a vote of 45 yeas to 44 nays, the Vice President casting the deciding vote.[57]

On June 21 the Bristow amendment was sent to the House and Mr. Olmstead, of Pennsylvania, moved that the House concur therewith.[58] Mr. Cullop, of Indiana, contended that the Bristow amendment was entirely unnecessary as section 5 of Article I, which declares that "Each House shall be the judge of the elections, returns, and qualifications of its own Members," is sufficient to control the election of Senators.[59]

The motion to concur was defeated, 111 yeas to 171 nays.[60] The Senate insisting on its amendment, and the House insisting on its original resolution, conferees were appointed by the respective Houses June 27 and July 5, and the entire matter went to conference.[61]

---

[56] Cong. Rec., vol. 47, pt. 2, p. 1482.

[57] Cong. Rec., vol. 47, pt. 2, pp. 1428, 1482–1490, 1879–1923.

[58] Cong. Rec., vol. 47, pt. 3, p. 2404.

[59] Ibid., p. 2408.

[60] Ibid., p. 2433.

[61] Ibid., pp. 2548–2549.

Over nine months later Senator Clark, of Wyoming, one of the Senate conferees, reported to the Senate that although 16 conferences had been held no agreement could be reached between the views of the respective Houses, and asked for further instructions. By a vote of 42 yeas to 36 nays the Senate on April 23, 1912, instructed the Senate conferees to insist on the Senate amendment.[62]

On April 26 Mr. Rucker, the author of the original resolution, informed the House that as the Senate was apparently adamant on its amendment, and that a further insistence on the part of the House on the original resolution was useless, and would only mean the failure of the entire measure, he recommended that the House recede from its disagreement to the Bristow amendment and concur in the same.[63] Some resentment was manifested by this withdrawal, but as conciliation was necessary in order to save the main principle, which was the direct election of Senators, the amendment was finally agreed to May 13, 1912, by a vote of 238 yeas to 39 nays. A last attempt to add a proviso to the measure, declaring that the " Congress shall not have the power or authority to provide for the qualification of electors of United States Senators, or to use supervision or force " at the polls during the said election was decisively defeated, 89 yeas to 189 nays.[64]

On May 16, 1912, the amendment was proposed to the legislatures of the several States, and on May 31, 1913, the Secretary of State declared that since it had been accepted by 36 of the 48 States it had been duly ratified, and

[62] Cong. Rec., Apr. 23, 1912, p. 5172.

[63] Cong. Rec., Apr. 23, 1912, p. 5172.

[64] Cong. Rec., May 13, 1912, pp. 6366–6367.

thus became the seventeenth amendment to the Constitution.[65]

In June, 1926, Mr. Rubey, of Missouri, introduced a resolution designed to prevent senatorial candidates from spending more than $10,000 for their nomination and election. This resolution was prompted by the disclosures of the large amounts spent in the spring of 1926 in the various primaries throughout the State.[66]

92. The prohibition amendment.

The eighteenth amendment is the only amendment which deals with affairs entirely personal as opposed to governmental. Indeed, it may be truly said to be the only provision in the Constitution as it now stands which demands certain conduct on the part of the individual which is not by its nature necessarily required of all in the regulation of society. Taxation, suffrage, representation, administration, interstate regulation, and the other items under constitutional control are subjects which must be attended to by the Federal Government in order that a uniform, smoothly working system of political, business, and social intercourse may be worked out. But the establishment of national prohibition which particularly and definitely goes into each State, city, town, and home and demands certain conduct there means the exercise of a police power entirely new to the Federal Government. In giving up control over the liquor traffic to the Federal Government, the States gave up an exclusive privilege of the police power which definitely marks a precedent in constitutional jurisprudence.

---

[65] S. Doc. No. 12, 63d Cong., 1st sess., p. 57.

[66] App., No. 1297.

93. History of prohibition in the United States.[67]

The first State or territory prohibitory law was passed in 1843 by the Oregon territorial legislature but was repealed in 1848. Delaware passed a prohibition law in 1847 which was declared unconstitutional by the Supreme Court of that State in 1848. In 1849 New York passed a law prohibiting the granting of licenses to sell wines and spirituous liquors. In 1851 Maine passed what has been known as the Neal Dow law providing for state-wide prohibition. It was repealed in 1856 but reenacted in 1859. The enforcement of prohibition in Maine was very difficult, if not impossible, during the Civil War and immediately afterwards by reason of the national liquor license law adopted by Congress. This law was passed for the purpose of raising revenue, and it permitted Federal agents to license the liquor traffic in Maine even though the State prohibited the sale of liquor.

On July 24, 1869, at Mansfield, Ohio, the first political prohibition party was formed. On September 1, 1869, the National Prohibition Party was formed at Chicago. In 1872 this party put a candidate in the field who received a total of 5,607 votes for the presidency. The Woman's Christian Temperance Union, which was formed in 1874, combined with this party in 1884. In each succeeding election the party nominated national officers but never did it suceed in becoming a major party. In 1916 their candidate for President received 220,506 votes.

[67] The section is based mostly on material contained in the following books: Cherrington, Ernest H. The Evolution of Prohibition in the United States of America. Mida, William. Mida's Compendium (Liquor Laws). Tuttle. Liquor Laws. Encyclopedia Britannica, vol. 16, article on liquor laws.

In the meantime other States had taken up the question of prohibition. Vermont, in 1852, voted for a discontinuance of the liquor traffic, Connecticut did the same in 1854, New Hampshire in 1855, and later Massachusetts and Rhode Island followed suit. All of these States except Maine, however, repealed the prohibitory laws after a more or less prolonged trial, as did also the Middle Western States of Michigan, Iowa, Nebraska, and South Dakota. New York passed a prohibition law in 1855 but it was declared unconstitutional. On the other hand, in the removed section of the country the proposition of prohibition took firmer root, and by 1907 the States of Kansas, North Dakota, Georgia, and Oklahoma, as well as Maine, had officially abandoned the use of intoxicating liquors within their borders, and in 1909 the Southern States of Alabama, Mississippi, North Carolina, and Tennessee did the same.

Local option seems to have had its first trial in the United States in Indiana in 1832. Georgia followed in 1833, and many of the States which later tried out general prohibition and then abandoned it fell back on the local form. In 1881 Massachusetts adopted local option after extensive experiment with prohibition and ordinary forms of license, and that State then became a model for other States in local option laws.

State-wide prohibition did not travel across the country very rapidly. By 1910 it existed in only nine States (enumerated above). It was not until 1914 that any greater tendency toward state-wide prohibition manifested itself, with the exception of an amendment of the State constitution of West Virginia in 1912. But during the five years 1914–1919 half the States adopted state-wide prohibition, although they did not include some of the most populous States with large urban centers. In 1914 state-wide prohibition was adopted by Colorado, Oregon, Virginia, Washington; in 1915, by Alabama, Arizona, South Carolina; in 1916, by Arkansas, Idaho, Iowa, Michigan, Montana, Nebraska, South Dakota; in 1917, by the District of Columbia, Indiana, New Hampshire, New Mexico; in 1918, by Florida, Nevada, Ohio, Utah; in 1919, by Kentucky and Texas.

94. Prohibition legislation in Congress.

With the individual States voting differently on the question of the legality of the liquor traffic, conflicts in jurisdiction between Federal and State control over the transportation of liquor shipments were bound to occur. In the case of Leisy *v.* Hardin[68] the Supreme Court of the United States declared that despite the prohibition laws of Iowa that State did not have the right to interfere in any way with liquor shipments in interstate commerce, the regulation of which was within the exclusive power of Congress. The famous " original package " rule was here laid down. It declared that no article which had moved in interstate commerce was subject to the local laws of the State to which it was shipped until it had been incorporated into the general mass of the property of the State. This decision caused State lines to be ignored and thus permitted nonprohibition States to defy the laws governing prohibited territory by sending liquor directly to the consumer. This anomaly was quickly removed by the passage by Congress on August 8, 1890,

[68] 135 U. S. 100.

of the Wilson law, declaring that shipments of liquor "shall upon arrival" in prohibited territory "be subject to the operation and effect of the law of such State or Territory enacted in the exercise of its police powers.[69] Prohibition States were given further assistance from the Federal Government by the approval of a law on March 4, 1909, which required that all liquor packages should bear a mark indicating the nature of their contents, and prohibiting railroad companies from engaging in the business of purchasing or selling liquor in any way.[70] This aid was carried still further by a law passed in 1913 over the President's veto which forbade the shipment of intoxicating liquors from one State into another with the intention of violating any State law.[71] The last measure of this series of State aids was what became known as the "Reed bone-dry amendment," approved March 3, 1917, which excluded from the mails any liquor advertisement addressed to persons in dry territory.[72]

All this legislation was passed under the power given Congress by the interstate commerce clause of the Constitution. (Art. I, sec. 8, cl. 3.) But by other sections of the Constitution (Art. I, sec. 8, cl. 17, and Art. IV, sec. 3, cl. 2) Congress has exclusive jurisdiction over Federal territory and the District of Columbia, and while acting as a legislature for such geographical divisions may exercise police power as any sovereign State. Accordingly, in this capacity it passed a law prohibiting the manufacture or sale of intoxicating liquors in the Territories of

[69] Public No. 235, 51st Cong., 1st sess.
[70] Public No. 350, 60th Cong., S. 2982.
[71] Public No. 398, 62d Cong., S. 403.
[72] Public No. 380, 64th Cong.

Alaska and Porto Rico.[73] It also established prohibition in the District of Columbia.[74]

During the War Congress passed a law prohibiting liquor in Army camps and forbidding its sale to soldiers anywhere.[75] Further war legislation on this subject prohibited the use of fruits and food materials for the manufacture of distilled spirits for beverage purposes and gave the President power to commandeer distilled spirits for redistillation.[76]

This activity in liquor legislation indicated that a majority of Congress favored the principle of prohibition, but not necesarily also the application of it to all the people by a Federal amendment. A large number of the legislators who advocated prohibition in the respective States were opposed to a Federal amendment on the ground that it would deprive the people in nonprohibition States of the right to decide for themselves a question which so directly affected their personal welfare.

95. Attempts made to add a prohibition amendment to the Constitution.

In September, 1876, Senator Blair, of New Hampshire, introduced in Congress the first prohibition amendment. At this time Maine appeared to be the only State seriously active in the attempt to abolish the liquor traffic and she submitted a resolution to Congress recommending the passage of this amendment.[77] From 1876 to 1913

[73] Public No. 308, 64th Cong., S. 7963; Public No. 368, 64th Cong.

[74] Public No. 388, 64th Cong., S. 1082.

[75] Public No. 12, 65th Cong.; Public No. 41, 65th Cong., made this apply also to sailors.

[76] Public No. 41, 65th Cong.

[77] Ames, p. 272.

prohibition amendments were presented sporadically (19 in all), but outside of a few zealous proponents of nation-wide prohibition very little attention was paid to them, as it seemed to be quite generally assumed that the control of the liquor traffic was a police power of the State which the Federal Government should not encroach upon.[78]

As dry territory commenced to expand, however, more and more Representatives were sent to Congress bound to accept prohibition as an established fact, and who were prevailed upon by prohibition workers to push Congress for a Federal amendment on the subject. Thus in the Sixty-third Congress there were proposed 14 resolutions declaring for an abolishment of the liquor traffic.[79] Twelve such amendments were introduced in the Sixty-fourth Congress [80] and 13 in the Sixty-fifth.[81]

In the pulpits, in the press, and in the legislatures throughout the country the advocates of prohibition heralded their cause. Opinions of medical scientists showing that liquor was of a permanently injurious nature taken in ever so little quantities were broadcast and had their effect.[82] Statistics were introduced to show the economic waste through the use of foodstuffs in the manufacturing of intoxicating beverages.[83]

Figures were presented showing how various commercial organizations, especially the railroads, forbade the

---

[78] Ames, pp. 272–273; see Appendix.

[79] See Appendix.

[80] See Appendix.

[81] Cong. Rec., vol. 55, pt. 6, p. 5549.

[83] Ibid., p. 5551.

use of liquor by their employees.[84] Petitions numbering into the millions were directed to Congress praying for the Federal abolition of intoxicating liquors.[85] This last fact led to the argument, vigorously advanced, that such legislators who were not in favor of the prohibition amendment should vote for its passage by Congress anyhow, so that the people might have an opportunity to pass upon the issue. A Senate report on the subject stated that—

> The method provided in the Constitution for its own peaceful amendment would be destroyed by failure to submit the proposition for amendment in cases of grave moment involving the approval and prayers of multitudes of the people, for where the remedy sought is admitted to be without the jurisdiction of the fundamental law, the petition is really addressed to the only tribunal which can enlarge that jurisdiction—that is to say, to the States themselves. Should, then, Congress in such case refuse to submit the proposal to the States, such refusal would constitute a substantial denial of the right of petition itself.[86]

The opponents of such an amendment declared that it was entirely without the letter and spirit of the Constitution; that there are certain matters in which "the authority of a State is complete, unqualified, and exclusive. Without attempting to define what are the peculiar subjects or limits of this power, it may safely be affirmed that every law for the restraint and punishment of crime, for the preservation of the public peace, health, and morality must come within this category."[87]

---

[84] Cong. Rec., vol. 55, pt. 6, p. 5593.

[85] Ibid., p. 5552.

[86] S. Rept. No. 52, p. 2, 65th Cong., 1st sess., quoting S. Rept. No. 1727, 50th Cong., 1st sess.

[87] H. Rept. No. 1493, pt. 2, 64th Cong., 2d sess.

Another objection was that universal prohibition would mean the destruction of much private property without compensation and that, assuming this could be done by a constitutional amendment, although not by a congressional act, that did not change the principle involved.[88]

It was also declared that under the present method of ratifying proposed amendments it was possible the amendment in question would be ratified without the consent of the States representing a majority of the population of the United States. Thus, 36 of the smaller States, with a combined smaller population than that of the 12 larger States, could enforce an undesired prohibition on the majority of the population. Further, "if the Federal Government is once called on to enter the field, apprehend, and punish the petty vices of the citizens of the States," as would be called for in a Federal prohibition amendment, "it will not be long before efforts will be made to further extend the police powers of the Federal Government and result in destroying State boundaries and the abolition of State governments." [89]

96. The eighteenth amendment.

On April 14, 1917, Senator Sheppard, for the fifth time, introduced a resolution proposing that the Constitution be amended so as to abolish the liquor traffic throughout the United States.[90] For the first time in the history of constitutional amendments a section was added declaring the period during which the amendment could be voted

[88] Cong. Rec., vol. 55, pt. 6, p. 5623.

[89] Ibid., p. 5555.

[90] App., No. 899.

on by the States. Senator Harding was the author of the original motion on this point, which read:

> This article shall be inoperative unless it shall have been ratified as an amendment to the Constitution by the legislatures of the several States, as provided in the Constitution, on or before the 1st day of July, A. D. 1923.[91]

Senator Sheppard suggested the time limit should be modified so that the clause would read " within six years from the date of its submission by the Congress," which substitution was accepted.[92] Senator Borah, of Idaho, doubted that this limitation could be of effect, as Article V of the Constitution stated a proposed amendment would become effective " when ratified," implying that the offer of an amendment once made could not be recalled.[93] Senator Cummins, of Iowa, in order to avoid any possible later controversy on the subject, and at the same time provide a limit to the time within which a State might ratify, proposed an amendment to Article V itself, declaring that proposed amendments must be ratified within a period of eight years after submission to be effective. He later withdrew this, and the 6-year section proposed by Senator Harding and amended by Senator Sheppard was accepted by the Senate.[94]

Senator Hardwick, who was opposed to the resolution, moved to add to the inhibitions of " manufacture, sale, and transportation " of intoxicating liquors, that of " purchase," thus to make more difficult the passage of the resolution. His amendment was rejected, 4 yeas to 62 nays.[95]

[91] Cong. Rec., vol. 55, pt. 6, p. 5648.

[92] Cong. Rec., ibid., p. 5649.

[93] Ibid., p. 5649.

[94] Cong. Rec., vol. 55, pt. 6, p. 5648.

[95] Ibid., p. 5648.

Senator Stone, of Missouri, moved to amend the resolution by adding:[96]

but this article shall not be enforced until the Congress shall have made provision for the ascertainment and payment of damages to the property employed in the manufacture of said liquors resulting from the enforcement of this article.

And Senator Brandegee added still further: "under such rules of evidence as Congress may provide." This combined amendment was defeated, 31 yeas to 50 nays.[97]

Senator Phelan, in order to save the wine industries of California, moved to substitute the words "distilled spiritous liquors" for "intoxicating liquors." Senator New made a like amendment. They were both rejected. The resolution as finally accepted by the Senate on August 1, 1917, by a vote of 65 yeas to 20 nays, read as follows:[98]

SECTION 1. The manufacture, sale, or transportation of intoxicating liquors within, the importation thereof into, or the exportation thereof from the United States and all territory subject to the jurisdiction thereof for beverage purposes is hereby prohibited.

SEC. 2. This article shall be inoperative unless it shall have been ratified as an amendment to the Constitution by the legislatures of the several States, as provided in the Constitution, within six years from the date of the submission hereof to the States by the Congress.

SEC. 3. The Congress shall have power to enforce this article by appropriate legislation.

In the House Judiciary Committee the resolution was amended to have the first section begin: "After one year from the ratification of this article, the," etc. Section 2 was made to read:

The Congress and the several States shall have concurrent power to enforce this article by appropriate legislation.

96 Cong. Rec., vol. 55, pt. 6, p. 5661.

97 Ibid., p. 5663.

98 Ibid., p. 5666.

Section 3 was substituted for the original section 2 and the ratifying time was extended to seven years.[99]

Mr. Webb, of North Carolina, from the Judiciary Committee, explained that the committee favored the new section 2 so that Congress might not take away from the various States the right to enforce their own prohibition laws. Also, to prevent "a fight in Congress every two years as to whether the States should be given the right to help enforce this proposed article of the Constitution." Further, it would avoid the necessity of employing extraordinarily large Federal forces to enforce the prohibition law when the States already have their own officers who are ready and willing to do so. The extension of the ratification time to seven years and the inclusion of the 1-year grace period were made to give the liquor interests a longer time in which to make arrangements for winding up their business should the amendment be ratified.[1]

In an effort to save the wineries of California, Mr. Lea, of that State, moved the adoption of an amendment:[2]

> *Provided,* This section shall not apply to wines containing not more than 14 per cent of alcohol or to beer containing not more than 3 per cent of alcohol, and the power to permit, regulate, and prohibit the manufacture, use, and sale of which is reserved to the separate States.

This amendment was defeated—107 yeas to 232 nays.

Mr. Steele moved the addition of another section to read:

> Any State may recall its rejection or ratification of this amendment at any time before three-fourths of the States have actually ratified the same.

---

[99] Cong. Rec., vol. 56, pt. 1, 423.

[1] Ibid., p. 424.

[2] Ibid., p. 469.

This amendment was also rejected. On the resolution itself the vote was 282 yeas to 128 nays. Two-thirds having thus voted in the affirmative, the resolution was passed.[3]

The amendment was proposed to the several States on December 18, 1917, and on January 29, 1919, the Secretary of State declared it to have been ratified by 36 States, and declared it to be in effect on January 16, 1920.[4]

97. Repeal of prohibition.

It can not be expected that a question on which a strong minority feel so deeply as the prohibition question can be settled instantaneously even by an amendment to the Constitution. Some of the people felt, in addition, that the method of proposal and ratification of the Eighteenth amendment was unfair in that it left them without a direct vote on a matter of such personal importance. Mr. Haskell, of New York, sensed this agitation and reflected it in an amendment proposed by him on May 19, 1919, which provided for a referendum on the question of prohibition, a majority vote to determine whether or not beverages of an intoxicating nature should be permitted in the United States.[5] On the same day he also introduced an amendment designed to repeal the eighteenth amendment by declaring that the liquor traffic should be permitted in the United States.[6]

On May 29, 1924, Mr. O'Sullivan, of Connecticut, introduced an amendment declaring categorically that the

[3] Cong. Rec., vol. 56, pt. 1, p. 470.

[4] World Almanac, 1922, p. 424.

[5] App., No. 973.

[6] App., No. 974.

Eighteenth amendment should be and "the same is hereby repealed."[7] In December, 1925, Mr. Hill, of Maryland, and, in January, 1927, Mr. Cochran, of Missouri, introduced similar resolutions.[8]

In the beginning of the first session of the Seventieth Congress Mr. Cochran again introduced this measure,[9] and in the same session, in April, 1928, Mr. Clancy, of Michigan, presented an identical resolution.[10]

Another proposition which gained a great deal of prominence was that although spirituous liquors were universally considered injurious and should be prohibited for beverage purposes, yet a majority of the people were in favor of light wines and beers. On this subject Mr. O'Connell, of New York, recommended an amendment providing for a referendum on the question:

> Shall the manufacture, sale, or transportation of beer, wine, and other malt or vinuous liquor within, the transportation thereof into, or the exportation thereof from the United States and all territory under its jurisdiction for beverage purposes be prohibited?[11]

This resolution was reintroduced by others in 1921 and 1923.[12]

On May 2, 1922, Mr. Ansorge, of New York, introduced two amendments on this subject, one declaring that the words " intoxicating liquors " in Article 18 of the Constitution shall not include wines or vinuous liquors containing less than 10 per cent of alcohol by volume or beers containing less than 2¾ per cent.[13] The other men-

[7]App., No. 1247.
[8]App., Nos. 1266, 1303.
[9]App., No. 1310.
[10]App., No. 1353.
[11]App., No. 1008.
[12]App., Nos. 1042, 1197
[13]App., No. 1101.

tioned only beers.[14] Both amendments provided that the individual States, but not Congress, had the power to reduce the alcoholic content of liquors mentioned in the resolutions. Further, that the amendments were not to become operative until they had been ratified by the legislatures of the several States, after an intervening election of members of the State legislatures and within seven years from the date of submission thereof to the States by Congress.[15]

In 1922 and 1923, two similar resolutions were introduced providing that upon ratification of the article by the legislatures of three-fourths of the States and a majority vote of the electors of the several States, the sale of 5 per cent beer should be permitted. Further, that the eighteenth amendment could be further amended or repealed only upon majority vote of the electors of the land.[16]

In December, 1925, in March, 1926, and again in December, 1927, Senator Bruce, of Maryland, introduced a resolution giving Congress power to regulate but not prohibit or unreasonably restrict the manufacture, sale, transportation, importation, or exportation of intoxicating liquors; also that, with the approval of the State legislatures, any political subdivision of a State could prohibit the traffic in liquor within the territorial limits thereof.[17]

On March 11, 1926, and again in December, 1927, Mr. Oliver, of New York, presented a resolution declaring that when a State law is consistent with the general

[14] App., No. 1102.
[15] Ibid.
[16] App., Nos. 1124, 1161.
[17] App., Nos. 1283, 1292, 1332.

purpose of the eighteenth amendment it shall be superior, within the territorial limits of that State, to any law of Congress in conflict therewith.[18]

On June 30, 1926, Senator Edwards, of New Jersey, and Mr. Gallivan, of Massachusetts, introduced resolutions in their respective Houses providing that the eighteenth amendment shall be repealed, the repeal to be ratified by conventions in three-fourths of the States, such conventions to take place prior to the 1928 presidential nominating conventions.[19]

Mr. LaGuardia, of New York, in the second session of the Sixty-ninth Congress, designed a constitutional amendment which would leave to the individual States the right to determine the alcoholic content of intoxicating beverages, and which would authorize Congress to establish the minimum alcoholic content of nonintoxicating beverages. There was a further provision in his resolution, which was introduced on December 23, 1926, that any State which fixed a greater alcoholic content than the minimum established by Congress could do so only under such laws and regulations as Congress "shall make and under such conditions as Congress shall impose to protect and guarantee other States adopting the minimum alcoholic content fixed by Congress from importations, sale, and traffic of such intoxicating beverages from such State."[20] He reintroduced this resolution in the first session of the Seventieth Congress.[21]

Mr. Cochran, of Missouri, presented on January 4, 1927, and again on December 5, 1927, a resolution declar-

[18] App., Nos. 1290.

[19] App., Nos. 1298, 1299, 1320.

[20] App., No. 1301.

[21] App., No. 1330.

ing that beverages obtained by the alcoholic fermentation of barley, malt, cereals, and hops in water, or by natural fermentation of fruits or vegetables containing not more than 3 per cent alcohol by volume, " may be manufactured, sold, or transported for sale in original packages for consumption in homes and places other than the place of sale." [22]

On February 22, 1927, Senator Edge, of New Jersey, presented an amendment to the Constitution which would authorize private persons within any State, Territory, or possession, to manufacture intoxicating liquors under Federal authority, supervision, and restrictions.[23]

The last amendment on the subject introduced in the Sixty-ninth Congress was one presented by Mr. Phillips, of Pennsylvania. His amendment provided that Congress shall have power to regulate and prohibit the liquor traffic, but that the several States shall not be " deprived of any of their regulatory or prohibitory power." [24]

In the first session of the Seventieth Congress, Senator Edwards, of New Jersey, proposed the repeal of the eighteenth amendment, the said repeal to become effective when ratified by conventions in three-fourths of the several States. His resolution stipulated that the conventions must be held prior to the 1930 congressional elections; further, that the delegates to the said conventions were to be elected by a majority in each State of the qualified voters thereof; and that the number of the delegates and the time and place of the conventions were to be determined by the respective State legislatures.[25]

[22]App., Nos. 1302, 1311.
[23]App., No. 1306.
[24]App., No. 1307.
[25]App., No. 1326.

On December 14, 1927, Mr. McLeod, of Michigan, submitted a resolution which would modify the eighteenth amendment so as to permit the manufacture and transportation of intoxicating beverages intended for use "in the home and places of abode."[26]

Mr. Sabath, of Illinois, in a resolution described as an amendment of the eighteenth amendment, proposed on December 15, 1927, that Congress be empowered to provide means for establishing Federal dispensaries for intoxicating liquors with the provision that it shall not establish dispensaries "in any State or Territory where intoxicating liquors are prohibited by law, nor in any municipality unless demanded by a majority vote at any special or regular election."[27]

On February 13, 1928, Mr. Sabath introduced another resolution on the same subject, this time proposing that Congress should have power to provide for the manufacture and transportation of intoxicating liquors under a system of governmental permits and restrictions. He added in this resolution an inhibition similar to the one contained in his previous resolution, namely, that Congress should not permit the issuance of governmental permits in any State or Territory where laws prohibit intoxicating beverages, nor in any political subdivision of the United States (outside the District of Columbia) until requested by an act of the legislature or referendum vote of such political subdivision.[28]

98. Woman suffrage.

The adoption of the nineteenth amendment to the Consituation, prohibiting the denial of the suffrage on account of sex, came as the culmination of over half a century's

[26] App., No. 1334.
[27] App., No. 1335.
[28] App., No. 1348.

efforts for the universal enfranchisement of women. From January 23, 1866, to June 4, 1919, no less than 118 amendments providing for woman suffrage were introduced in Congress, and the final adoption came only after a most prolonged and bitter contest as to the feasibility and wisdom of further restricting the States in their sovereign right to determine the qualifications of their electors. In order to show how this amendment was at last inevitable I will give a brief history of the suffrage movement in this country, indicating its progress from section to section until, in 1919, 41 of the 48 States had in some form and to some degree granted women the right of the ballot.

99. History of the suffrage movement in the States.[29]

Passing over the negligible instance of New Jersey, where, from 1776 to 1807, on account of an oversight in the Constitution, women in that State had the right to vote, the question of woman suffrage did not assume any great public importance until after the Civil War. In 1869 two national organizations were formed pledged to work for universal suffrage—the National Women's Suffrage Association, in New York, and the American Woman's Suffrage Association, in Cleveland. In the same year the Legislature of the Territory of Wyoming passed a measure conferring the privilege of the ballot upon its women.[30]

---

[29] The section giving the history of the suffrage movement in the States is based mostly on material contained in the book entitled "A Brief History of the Movement for Woman Suffrage," by Ida Husted Harper, and the book, "Woman Suffrage by Federal Constitutional Amendment," by Carrie Chapman Catt.

[30] Bryce, II, p. 553. It has been claimed that the bill granting the suffrage was pushed through by means of a strategem and that the legislature as a whole did not really intend passing it.

Two other Territories, Utah and Washington, also attempted to give their women the right of suffrage, but their laws in this respect were nullified—the former by a Federal statute, because it was thought the measure was passed to increase the political strength of the Mormons with their numerous wives, and the latter by a decision of the United States Territorial Court declaring that the act of Congress organizing the Washington Territory did not authorize its legislature to enfranchise women.

Although the next full grant of the franchise to the women of a State did not come until 1893, many States in the meantime passed legislation permitting their women to vote on certain issues. It may be stated in passing that the State of Kentucky as early as 1838 had permitted women to vote at elections of school officers or on some question connected with schools. In 1875 the State of Minnesota granted these same privileges to the women within its borders, followed by New Hampshire in 1878, Massachusetts in 1879, Mississippi in 1880, New Jersey in 1887, and Connecticut in 1893. During the last year mentioned the Legislature of Colorado submitted to her people the question of granting complete franchise for all purposes to women. The People's Party, which favored woman suffrage, was at this time making heavy inroads upon the old party organizations, and it appears that this party, with the aid of the Knights of Labor and other workmen's organizations declaring for political equality, was most responsible for the majority vote of 6,347 with which the proposal became a law.

Although the suffrage organizations were disseminating a great deal of propaganda during this period, and there was much surface agitation in favor of woman suffrage, it does not appear that the women themselves as a whole were very much interested as to whether they got the vote or not. In States where they had been given the full or partial vote they were generally apathetic as to its use. There was always, of course, the small minority which made up in vigor what it did not have in numbers, and these few were able to keep the flag flying inviting those of nonsuffrage States to take up the good cause. There was also the growing opinion among the male citizens that whether or not woman suffrage would better civic conditions, as a matter of abstract right the women as citizens should have the ballot if they wanted it.

In 1896 Utah and Idaho granted the full suffrage to the women of those States. In 1894 Iowa and Ohio, in 1898 Delaware and Louisiana, and in 1900 Wisconsin, respectively, empowered the women therein to vote on school or tax measures. At this point the peak seemed to have been reached, as there was no further extension of the suffrage until 1910. Commencing with 1910, however, the tide once more rose and it slowly and effectively commenced to move across the country. New Mexico granted partial suffrage to her women and Washington full suffrage in that year. Then came the following States, all yielding full privileges of the ballot to their citizens without regard to sex: California in 1911; Kansas, Arizona, and Oregon in 1912; Nevada and Montana in 1914; New York in 1917; Michigan, Oklahoma, and South Dakota in 1918; Texas and Tenessee in 1919. The privilege of voting at presidential and municipal elections was given by the following States in the years indicated: Illinois in 1913; Nebraska and North Dakota, 1917; Indiana, 1919. For presidential elections only the privilege was given by

Rhode Island in 1917, and by Iowa, Tennessee, Vermont, Wisconsin, Maine, Minnesota, and Missouri in 1919. Primary suffrage was given to the women in Arkansas in 1917 and in Texas in 1918.[31]

100. Woman suffrage in the National Legislature.

To Mr. Brooks, of New York, goes the honor of having introduced the first woman suffrage amendment. This was presented in 1866 in the form of an amendment to one of the resolutions which later became part of the fourteenth amendment. Mr. Brooks had received and he then presented to Congress a petition from several thousand woman suffragists, with the proposal that the pending resolution be amended to read:

> That whenever the elective franchise shall be denied or abridged in any State on account of race or color or sex, all persons therein of such race or color or sex shall be excluded from the basis of representation.[32]

In 1869 Mr. Brooks again offered a substitution for the then pending suffrage resolution, proposing that it should read:

> The right of any person of, the United States to vote shall not be denied or abridged by the United States or any State by reason of his or her race, sex, nativity, or age when over 12 years, color or previous condition of slavery of any citizen or class of citizens of the United States.

Senator Pomeroy, of Kansas, also endeavored in vain at this time to include in the suffrage amendments a provision guaranteeing the franchise to women.[33]

---

[31] Cong. Rec., 66th Cong., 1st sess., vol. 58, pt. 1, p. 84.

[32] Ames, p. 237.

[33] Ibid., p. 238.

The first definite report on a suffrage amendment was made in the second session of the Forty-fifth Congress on a resolution introduced by Senator Sargent, of California, on January 10, 1878. The report was adverse to the passage of the resolution, as was also the next report on this subject, which was rendered in the first session of the Forty-ninth Congress on a resolution presented by Mr. Reed of Maine. The proposal was brought to a vote for the first time on January 25, 1887, and was rejected by the Senate, 16 yeas to 34 nays. The resolution was that of Senator Blair, of New Hampshire, who presented five amendments in all on this subject.[34] One of these amendments was of a penalizing nature and stipulated that the representation in Congress of any State refusing to grant woman suffrage should be halved in consequence thereof.[35]

Commencing with the Fortieth Congress and continuing to the Sixty-first Congress, inclusive (with the exception of the Forty-third and Forty-fourth, during which no such amendment was presented), from one to four amendments providing for the enfranchisement of women were introduced during each Congress.[36] In 1911, however, the real flood of suffrage amendments began. This was practically contemporaneous with the starting of a general movement throughout the States for women enfranchisement. Seven proposals for universal suffrage were introduced during the Sixty-second Congress[37] and a like number in the Sixty-third.[37] During the Sixty-fourth Congress this number increased to 14.[37] A simi-

[34] Ames, p. 238.

[35] App., No. 43.

[36] Ames, p. 238. See Appendix.

[37] See Appendix.

lar number of amendments were presented in the first session alone of the Sixty-fifth Congress,[38] nine during the second session,[38] and five in the third session.[38] On May 19, 1919, the Sixty-sixth Congress was convened in extraordinary session, and it was generally understood that a suffrage amendment would be proposed and doubtlessly favorably voted upon. In 10 days 14 amendments on the subject were presented.[38]

Out of all these proposals only seven distinct votes were taken on the suffrage amendment. The first vote has already been mentioned. The second was also in the Senate. It was on the resolution introduced by Senator Chamberlain of Oregon, which was defeated on March 19, 1919, by a vote of 35 yeas, 34 nays.[39] On January 10, 1918, the House passed the Raker amendment, 174 yeas to 136 nays.[40] The Senate rejected this amendment twice—once on October 1, 1918, 53 yeas to 31 nays, and again on February 10, 1919, 55 yeas to 29 nays.[41] The last two votes will be discussed in the section covering the amendment as finally passed.[42]

101. Arguments for and against a Federal suffrage amendment.

It was held by the Supreme Court in the case of Minor *v.* Happersett[43] that while citizenship was not dependent upon sex, and that therefore a woman could be a citizen, that this citizenship did not of itself confer upon the woman, or man either, the right to vote. The States in

[38] See Appendix.

[39] App., S. J. Res. 1, 63d Cong., 1st sess.

[40] App., No. 938.

[41] Ibid.

[42] Sec. 102.

[43] 21 Wall. 162.

their sovereign power can establish such qualifications for the suffrage as they choose, so long as they do not deprive a United States citizen of the suffrage privilege merely on account of "race, color, or previous condition of servitude." (Fourteenth amendment.) Nothing short of a Federal amendment could therefore guarantee the women of the United States the privilege of the ballot.

On the conviction that since it was within the power of every State to extend the suffrage should its citizens so desire, many of the legislators commenting on the proposed Federal amendment specifically stated that, while in favor of the principle of woman suffrage, they would not vote to further limit the powers of the State. The platforms of the Republican and Democratic Parties of 1916 declared in favor of woman suffrage, but indicated it should be secured through State action. President Wilson was also of this opinion, although he changed in 1919.

The greatest objections to a Federal suffrage amendment came from the southern delegations in Congress. They complained that it would open up again the negro question. Mr. Clark, of Florida, speaking on this proposition said:

> Make this amendment a part of the Federal Constitution and the negro women of the Southern States, under the tutelage of the fast-growing socialistic element of our common country, will become fanatical on the subject of voting and will reawaken in the negro men an intense and not easily quenched desire to again become a political factor.[44]

On this subject Senator Smith, of South Carolina, said:

> In our dual form of government the principle of its quality is the one that makes it possible for every part of this vast domain of ours

[44] Cong. Rec., vol. 58, pt. 1, p. 90.

to progress as conditions justify. Were we a homogeneous people, were the local conditions, both social, commercial, and industrial, the same, it might be less destructive of the spirit of democracy to adopt such an amendment.[45]

It was frankly stated by some of the legislators that the concentration of efforts for universal suffrage should be directed toward Congress, for it was easier to get through a Federal amendment than to secure favorable action in the respective States. "Practical experience and long study has taught the women that the State way is rough, untraveled, and all but impassible."[46]

In a Senate report on one of these amendments it was declared that the precedent for interfering with State rights in the matter of suffrage had already been made, and that inasmuch as the "Nation nearly half a century ago determined to restrict State authority over the ballot by abolishing certain disqualifications theretofore prevailing, it seems but appropriate and desirable that it should emphasize that policy by abolishing the disqualification of sex, a disqualification affecting 50 per cent of our population and far less defensible than those enumerated in the fifteenth amendment. It would equalize political conditions throughout the country, negatively at least, thus removing one of the greatest sources of existing popular discontent."[47]

In a report rendered December 18, 1917, on the woman suffrage amendment then under consideration, Mr. Dyer, of Missouri, asserted that it should be passed because it "is a war measure of the most definite sort."[48]

[45] Cong. Rec., vol. 58, pt. 1, p. 618.

[46] H. Rept. No. 1216, pt. 2, 64th Cong., 2d sess.

[47] S. Rept. No. 35, 64th Cong., 1st sess.

[48] Cong. Rec., vol. 56, pt. 1, p. 794.

102. The nineteenth amendment.

On May 19, 1919, Mr. Mann, of Illinois, introduced the resolution which became H. J. Res. No. 1 and later the nineteenth amendment. It read as follows: [49]

The right of citizens of the United States shall not be denied or abridged by the United States or by any State on account of sex.

Congress shall have power to enforce this article by appropriate legislation.

President Wilson, in his message to Congress, referring to this subject, said:

It seems to me that every consideration of justice and of public advantage calls for the immediate adoption of that amendment and its submission forthwith to the legislatures of the several States.[50]

This statement of the President's crystallized pretty well the majority opinion in Congress and no time was lost in reporting the resolution from the House Committee on Woman Suffrage. On the 21st the House was ready to vote. Mr. Saunders, of Virginia, proposed that ratification of the amendment be by "popular vote in three-fourths of the several States," instead of by the legislatures as the resolution read.[51] This amendment was rejected, and the resolution itself was on May 21 passed by a vote of 304 yeas to 90 nays.[52]

In the Senate on May 23 an attempt was made to expedite the passage of the resolution by a motion on the part of Senator Jones, of Washington, to discharge the Senate Committee on Woman Suffrage, to which it had been referred, from further consideration thereof. Sen-

[49] App., No. 971.

[50] Cong. Rec., vol. 58, pt. 1, p. 69.

[51] Ibid., p. 87.

[52] Ibid., p. 93–94.

ator Underwood, of Alabama, complained that this was an attempt to railroad the resolution through and that some time should be given the committee for a proper consideration of the measure.[53] On May 28 the resolution was returned by the committee without amendment.[54]

Senator Harrison, of Mississippi, moved that the resolution be amended so that the first sentence would read: "The right of white citizens to vote," etc. This amendment was rejected by the Senate.[55] Senator Underwood, realizing also, as did Mr. Saunders in the House, that the amendment would have more difficulty of ratification by popular or convention vote than by the legislatures of the several States, moved that the form of ratification of the proposed amendment be by "conventions in three-fourths of the several States."[56] Senator Phelan, of California, suggested that should this provision be incorporated into the eventual resolution the legislatures of the States might delay indefinitely the calling of the required conventions, and accordingly moved to further amend the resolution by declaring that "such conventions shall be called to meet by the governors of the several States on the first Tuesday after the first Monday of September, 1919." This was rejected.[57] The Underwood amendment was then voted upon and defeated, 28 yeas to 55 nays.[58]

An amendment by Senator Gay, that "the several States shall have the authority to enforce this article by

[53] Cong. Rec., vol. 58, pt. 1, p. 227.

[54] Ibid., p. 348.

[55] Ibid., p. 557.

[56] Ibid., p. 567.

[57] Ibid., p. 633.

[58] Ibid., p. 633.

special legislation, but if any State shall enforce or enact any laws in conflict therewith, then Congress shall not be excluded from enacting proper legislation to enforce it," was also defeated. The resolution as originally presented was voted on June 4, 1919, and passed by a vote of 56 yeas to 25 nays.[59]

Having passed both Houses by the requisite two-thirds majority, it was sent to the States for ratification. The thirty-sixth State (Tennessee) ratified the amendment on August 18, 1920, when it officially went into effect.[60]

103. Equal rights of women.

In order evidently further to strengthen the political rights of women, two resolutions were introduced in 1923, two in 1925, and two in 1928 proposing that an amendment be added to the Constitution reading: "Men and women shall have equal rights throughout the United States and every place subject to its jurisdiction." [61]

---

[59] Cong. Rec., vol. 58, pt. 1, p. 635.
[60] World Almanac, 1922, p. 425.
[61] App., Nos. 1188, 1194, 1273, 1281, 1341, 1360.

ADDITIONAL COPIES
OF THIS PUBLICATION MAY BE PROCURED FROM
THE SUPERINTENDENT OF DOCUMENTS
U. S. GOVERNMENT PRINTING OFFICE
WASHINGTON, D. C.
AT
30 CENTS PER COPY (PAPER COVERS)
▽